THE DAILY PRESSFIELD

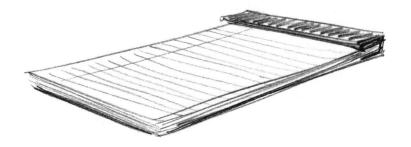

ALSO BY STEVEN PRESSFIELD

FICTION

The Legend of Bagger Vance
Gates of Fire
Tides of War
Last of the Amazons
The Virtues of War
The Afghan Campaign
Killing Rommel
The Profession
The Knowledge
36 Righteous Men
A Man at Arms

NONFICTION

The War of Art
Do the Work
The Warrior Ethos
Turning Pro
The Authentic Swing
The Lion's Gate
An American Jew
Nobody Wants to Read Your Sh*t
The Artist's Journey
Put Your Ass Where Your Heart Wants To Be
Govt Cheese: A Memoir

THE DAILY PRESSFIELD

A Teaching a Day from the Author of "The War of Art"

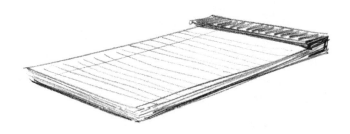

Illustrations by Victor Juhasz

Sarsaparilla Media LLC
Los Angeles, CA

THE DAILY PRESSFIELD

Steven Pressfield

Copyright © 2023 Steven Pressfield

Cover design by Diana Wilburn

For permission to reproduce selections from this book, write to:
Permissions, Sarsaparilla Media LLC
PO Box 2488, Malibu CA 90265

Hardback ISBN: 979-8-9878716-0-7
eBook ISBN: 979-8-9878716-2-1
Audiobook ISBN: 979-8-9878716-1-4
Paperback: ISBN: 979-8-9878716-3-8

Library of Congress Control Number: 2023910379
Printed in the United States of America.

www.stevenpressfield.com

10 9 8 7 6 5 4 3 2 1

For Ryan Holiday,
who gave me the idea...and the title.

"There is a second self inside you—an inner, shadow Self. This self doesn't care about you. It doesn't love you. It has its own agenda, and it will kill you. It will kill you like cancer. It will kill you to achieve its agenda, which is to prevent you from actualizing your Self, from becoming who you really are. This shadow self is called, in the Kabbalistic lexicon, the yetzer hara. *The yetzer hara, Steve, is what you would call Resistance."*

RABBI MORDECAI FINLEY, IN CONVERSATION
JULY 4, 2010

INTRODUCTION
ART = LIFE

Here's one thing you learn as a writer or an artist:

The stuff of our stories parallels the stuff of our lives.

Are we, like our heroes, lost? Are we afraid to launch ourselves after our dreams? Halfway there, are we seized by a nameless panic? Are we up against a villain? Is it ourselves?

Art parallels life. Why wouldn't it? The demons that our heroes duel in our dances, our songs, and our novels are the same demons you and I battle inside our heads in creating these dances, these songs, these novels.

You and I are the heroes of this coming year.

We're going to live it out—chasing our dreams and facing our demons—just like the protagonist of a novel or a dance or a movie.

Let's take these fifty-two weeks, then, and track them through, day by day, as we commit to our calling 24/7/365.

P.S. This is a through-the-year book but it's not a calendar. You don't have to wait for January 1 to start.

Day One is today.

Turn to it and begin.

WEEK ONE

RESISTANCE WAKES UP WITH ME

Day 1
RESISTANCE WAKES UP WITH ME

People ask me sometimes, "When in your day do you first experience Resistance?"

My answer: "The instant I open my eyes."

Maybe sooner.

Resistance is waiting for me.

It doesn't give me even .0001 second of slack.

BLACK IRISH JAB #22, "A DAY IN THE LIFE"

Resistance is a force of nature. I mean that literally.

Like gravity or the transit of the stars, Resistance operates objectively.

We can't evade it and we can't fake it out. The instant we surface to consciousness, it's there.

I've been in the writing biz for almost fifty years, and I can tell you:

Resistance never goes away.

It never diminishes.

The struggle for me is as difficult today as it was in 1974.

Let's make this, then, our hardball, hardcore assumption from Day One:

We will have to fight Resistance every day, all year long, from the moment we open our eyes.

Day 2
"GET UP! BEGIN YOUR DAY!"

I was listening to a recorded talk by Paramahansa Yogananda (1893–1952). He was recounting his own mental process first thing in the morning.

"Get up! Do not lie there 'thinking.' Nothing good ever came from that. Get up! Begin your day!"

When Yogananda says "thinking," I know exactly what he means.

He means Resistance.

Every second we lie there indulging it, we get weaker...and our resolve to do our work lessens.

"Get up! Do not lie there 'thinking.' Nothing good ever came from that. Get up! Begin your day!"

BLACK IRISH JAB #22, "A DAY IN THE LIFE"

One of Resistance's most diabolical tricks is to make us believe that its voice is "our" voice.

It ain't.

I've gotten thousands of letters and e-mails from writers and artists detailing the dialogue they hear inside their skulls.

Trust me, it's identical to the stuff you're hearing and the stuff I'm hearing.

Don't listen to it.

Get up! Begin your day!

Day 3
A GYM PERSON

I'm a gym person.

I go early. Ridiculously early.

And I work out hard. Ridiculously hard.

Why?

Because I'm rehearsing.

I'm rehearsing doing something I don't want to do.

I'm rehearsing doing something I'm afraid of.

I'm rehearsing doing something that hurts.

I'm rehearsing for the moment when I get to the keyboard and sit down to work.

"WRITING WEDNESDAYS," STEVENPRESSFIELD.COM, 10/9/19

My friend Randy Wallace, who wrote *Braveheart*, has a practice he calls "little successes."

He tries each morning to establish a sequence of endeavors that he can complete to his satisfaction. The run of successes (he counts brushing his teeth and taking a shower in that category) builds momentum. It gets his day rolling in a positive direction.

Like me, Randy is building up steam toward the moment when he has to close the door and get down to business.

Day 4
NO DISTRACTIONS

It goes without saying, I have turned off all external sources of distraction.

No phone.

No e-mail.

No Instagram.

No Facebook.

I'm on an ice floe in the Antarctic.

I'm circling alone at seventy thousand feet.

I'm on the moon.

Barring a nuclear attack or a family emergency, I will not while I'm working turn my attention to anything that's not happening inside my own demented skull.

BLACK IRISH JAB #22, "A DAY IN THE LIFE"

I've said for years that if you want to become an instant billionaire, invent something that makes it easy for people to succumb to the voice of Resistance in their heads.

Well, someone did invent it.

It's called the web.

It's called social media.

It's called going down the rabbit hole of distraction and clickbait.

Day 5
RESISTANCE COMES SECOND

Here's the good news:

Resistance comes second.

Resistance never appears alone. It comes only *as a response to a vision*, to a dream inside you and me. That dream is the book we want to write, the movie we want to make, the start-up we aim to get off the ground.

If there were no dream, there would be no Resistance.

Imagine a tree in the middle of a sunny meadow. The tree inevitably casts a shadow.

That tree is your dream.

Resistance is the shadow.

Never forget—the dream always comes first.

INTERVIEW WITH OPRAH WINFREY, SUPER SOUL SUNDAY, 9/20/13

In other words, if you find yourself experiencing intense Resistance, that's a good sign. It means that inside you a dream is calling, demanding your participation in helping it to be brought into material being.

Day 6
THE BIGGER THE DREAM,
THE STRONGER THE RESISTANCE

Like a magnetized needle floating on a surface of oil, Resistance will unfailingly point to true North—meaning that calling or action it most wants to stop us from doing.

Rule of thumb: the more important a call or action is to our soul's evolution, the more Resistance we will feel toward pursuing it.

THE WAR OF ART, P. 12

In other words, there's more good news.

The greater the Resistance we find ourselves experiencing, the bigger the dream percolating inside us.

Resistance operates like Newton's Third Law of Motion. For every action (our Dream), there is an equal and opposite Reaction (Resistance).

Big Resistance = Big Dream.

Day 7
RESISTANCE AND SELF-DOUBT

Self-doubt can be an ally. This is because it serves as an indicator of aspiration. It reflects love—love of something we dream of doing—and desire to do it. If you find yourself asking yourself (and your friends), "Am I a real writer? Am I a real artist?", chances are you are.

THE WAR OF ART, P. 39

Today is the last day of Week One. Let's end it on a note of reality and resolve.

Yes, we face an enemy—an enemy inside us.

And yes, that foe is implacable, insidious, indefatigable. It will never let up and never let go.

But the flip side is that the very presence of this enemy tells us our creative soul is being called to something wonderful, something we, and we alone, are capable of perceiving and that we, and we alone, are capable of producing.

We are in a war.

The war of art.

Let's win it.

STEVEN PRESSFIELD

WEEK TWO

BEFORE WE
WRITE THE FIRST WORD

Day 8
"HOW HARD CAN IT BE?"

In my early twenties I worked as a junior copywriter at a big Madison Avenue ad agency. My boss was a gentleman named Ed Hannibal.

One day Ed quit to write a novel.

The novel (*Chocolate Days, Popsicle Weeks*; you can look it up) was an instant success. Overnight Ed became famous. He was a star.

I thought, *Hell, I'll do the same thing. How hard can it be?*

I quit too.

I plunged in on my own novel.

Can you guess what's coming?

BLACK IRISH JAB #14, "COVER THE CANVAS"

I too was an instant success as a novelist. It just took me twenty-eight years longer than it took Ed.

Day 9
IT AIN'T BRAIN SURGERY.
IT'S HARDER.

Of course, the dream of making a living as a writer or an artist or an entrepreneur is a tremendous long shot. The odds are overwhelmingly against success, particularly if we set as our goal the ideal to be true to ourselves and to our unique gifts.

To say we want to succeed on such terms in the contemporary universe of competition is like saying we want to be a professional basketball player. It's easier to become a brain surgeon. At least you can go to school for that.

FROM A LETTER TO A READER, 2/6/20

How hard can it be? The answer is that's not the right question.

The right question is, "Do you have any choice?"

If you're a real writer or artist, you don't.

Day 10
BANANAS

I was living in the back of my Chevy van when I found myself, as night was falling, in a neighborhood in New Orleans that I didn't know. I had to find a place to pull over and sleep.

I turned in someplace dark and settled down for the night. When I woke the next morning, I realized I had parked in the lot of a banana importing company. I opened my side doors and stuck my head out.

In front of me, on the loading dock, was a big iron cage. In the cage was a gorilla. I guess he was the banana company's mascot.

Just at that moment, a workman came out from the back of the warehouse. He had two bananas in his hand.

He gave one banana to the gorilla and one banana to me. Then he turned around and went back into the warehouse.

He never said a word.

The gorilla and I sat there and enjoyed our bananas.

WRITING SEMINAR, NASHVILLE, 2019

Why was I in New Orleans? Because I had tried to write a hit novel like my boss Ed Hannibal and instead, about a week from the finish line, I blew the whole thing up. I was on the road, broke and lost.

I didn't know about Resistance then.

I had no idea there was such a thing.

STEVEN PRESSFIELD

Day 11
A KING

Once Alexander the Great was leading his army across a waterless desert. The column was strung out for miles, with men and horses suffering terribly from thirst.

Suddenly a detachment of scouts came galloping back to the king. They had found a small spring and had managed to fill a helmet with water. They rushed to Alexander and presented this to him. The army held in place, watching. Every man's eye was fixed upon the king. Alexander thanked his scouts for bringing him this gift. Then, without touching a drop, he lifted the helmet and poured the precious liquid into the sand.

At once a great cheer ascended, rolling from one end of the column to the other. A soldier was heard to say, "With a king like this to lead us, no force on earth can stand against us."

THE WARRIOR ETHOS, P. 42–43, PARAPHRASING PLUTARCH, LIFE OF ALEXANDER

Can we be the commanders of our own enterprise?

Can we embrace adversity and be willing to make the sacrifices necessary for our project to reach fruition?

Can we be the king (or queen) of our own aspirations?

Day 12
A HELLHOLE ON WHEELS

When I lived in the back of my Chevy van, I had to dig my type-writer out from beneath layers of tire tools, dirty laundry, and moldering paperbacks. My truck was a nest, a hive, a hellhole on wheels whose sleeping surface I had to clear each night just to carve out a foxhole to snooze in.

The professional cannot live like that. He is on a mission. He will not tolerate disorder. He eliminates chaos from his world in order to banish it from his mind.

He wants the carpet vacuumed and the threshold swept, so the Muse may enter and not soil her gown.

THE WAR OF ART, P. 77

Are you about to start your new novel? Screenplay? Thai fusion restaurant?

Now is the time to set your mind to the level of professionalism you will need to carry your vision through to completion.

Now is the time to start thinking of yourself not as an amateur but as a professional.

Day 13
TURNING PRO IS FREE

Turning pro is free, but it's not easy. When we turn pro, we give up a life that we may have become extremely comfortable with. We give up a self that we have come to identify with and to call our own.

Turning pro is free, but it demands sacrifice. The passage from amateur to professional is often achieved via an interior odyssey whose trials are survived only at great cost. We pass through a membrane when we turn pro. It's messy and it's scary. We tread in blood when we turn pro.

TURNING PRO, BACK COVER COPY

When we say "turn pro," we don't mean literally that from this day we will work only for money. We mean change our mindset.

An amateur approaches her work like an amateur. A pro approaches her work like a pro.

An amateur has amateur habits. A pro has professional habits.

You don't have to take a course or get a certificate to turn pro. All you have to do is change your mind.

Day 14
A KING, PART TWO

"I will tell His Majesty what a king is. A king does not abide within his tent while his men bleed and die upon the field. A king does not dine while his men go hungry, nor sleep when they stand at watch upon the wall. A king does not command his men's loyalty through fear nor purchase it with gold; he earns their love by the sweat of his own back and the pains he endures for their sake. That which comprises the harshest burden, a king lifts first and sets down last. A king does not require service of those he leads but provides it to them. He serves them, not they him."

GATES OF FIRE, P. 360 [HARDBACK]

As you and I set out on a new project, particularly the grueling, long-form kind—a novel, a screenplay, a start-up business—we need to connect first with the King or Queen archetype in our psyche.

When the king acts with wisdom and justice, the kingdom prospers. When the queen is in touch with her creative center, the kingdom flourishes and grows.

STEVEN PRESSFIELD

WEEK THREE

THE FOOLSCAP METHOD

Day 15
BEFORE DRAFT #1

Here we are, about to start writing our novel (or choreographing our dance or launching our nonprofit or inaugurating our start-up business).

But what do we do before that?

I mean the very first step.

How do we set sail for Tahiti? How do we fly to the moon? What's the first thing we do when we roll out of bed on the very first morning?

BLACK IRISH JAB #21, "THE FOOLSCAP METHOD"

For me, that step is to prepare a Foolscap Page.

Day 16
A LUNCH WITH MY MENTOR

I was having a cheeseburger with my friend and mentor, the writer and documentarian Norm Stahl. I was trying to start my first novel at the time, and I was dazed, confused, baffled, stumped, lost, perplexed, and desperate.

Norm happened to have a pad of yellow legal-sized foolscap paper in his briefcase. He took it out and set it on the table between us.

"Steve," Norm said, "God made a single sheet of yellow foolscap to be exactly the right length to hold the outline of an entire novel."

At one stroke, Norm knocked 99.99% of the preciousness out of me. He gave me a key to transforming myself from an amateur to a pro.

"WRITING WEDNESDAYS," STEVENPRESSFIELD.COM, 4/6/11

The genius of the Foolscap concept is that it forces us to boil down our enterprise to its absolute essentials. What remains is the pure essence of our book, our voyage to Bali, our campaign for elective office.

FOOLSCAPPING *MOBY DICK*

HERO: Captain Ahab, master of the whaling ship *Pequod*.

VILLAIN: The great White Whale, Moby Dick.

NARRATIVE DEVICE: Story told in recollection by Ishmael, sole survivor of the *Pequod*.

ACT ONE: *Pequod* sets out to sea.

ACT TWO: *Pequod* searches globe for Moby Dick.

ACT THREE: *Pequod* finds Moby Dick, duels him to the death.

BLACK IRISH JAB #21, "THE FOOLSCAP METHOD"

Moby Dick, in the copy in my library, is 589 pages. But all Herman Melville needed to start was a Foolscap like the one above.

From this single sheet, Melville could ask himself (and answer):

Is this an exciting story? Is it about something important? Will it work? Can I write it?

Day 18
ELEMENTS OF THE FOOLSCAP PAGE

Here are the headings I include on my Foolscap Page:

Genre.

Narrative device.

Theme.

Inciting Incident.

Act One, Act Two, Act Three.

Hero.

Villain.

Climax.

Did I always do this? No. The first three novels I wrote, I plunged in on Page One and didn't look up till THE END. That's right, I never found a publisher for those novels. That's right, none of the stories worked.

BLACK IRISH JAB #21, "THE FOOLSCAP METHOD"

Starting a book, I have sometimes done ridiculously detailed outlines. Sometimes I've worked like a screenwriter and prepared sixty index cards, one for each scene, and pinned them to the wall.

But I will never, *never* start on a new project without preparing a Foolscap Page first.

Day 19
WHY THE FOOLSCAP IS IMPORTANT

The Foolscap is critical because the act of compiling it forces us to *see the work as a whole.*

It gives us a snapshot and helps us to evaluate what we've got.

When we've completed our Foolscap and we sit down to read it over, we get a real sense of what our prospective book (or other enterprise) actually is.

Will it work?

Is it interesting?

Is it a worthwhile expenditure of our time?

Does it possess commercial viability?

BLACK IRISH JAB #21, "THE FOOLSCAP METHOD"

There's a term in the movie biz called a "log line." It's like the nutshell descriptions you see in the TV Guide section of a newspaper.

"Private eye fights zombies in post-apocalyptic Manhattan."

A Foolscap Page is like that, only more helpful. Because it's so short, we can see our project at a glance and evaluate it. But because its constituent elements cross-dissect the story, we also get a kind of 3-D X-ray of how the damn thing works (or doesn't).

Day 20
A FOOLSCAP FORCES US TO ANSWER THE BIG QUESTIONS

If you're like me, you tend to fall in love with one specific element of a new idea and want to plunge in, based on that emotional notion alone.

Maybe we become smitten with one killer scene.

Maybe we hook ourselves with the character of the hero or heroine.

Or we become enamored of a theme, or a wonderful quirky twist, or a thermonuclear ending.

This is not good.

It's not good because three months into the project we will come to our senses and realize we've got half-a-story or part-of-a-novel.

Executing a Foolscap Page saves us from that.

BLACK IRISH JAB #21, "THE FOOLSCAP METHOD"

If the Foolscap works, there's a good chance the completed story will work. If it doesn't, nothing we can do will save it.

Day 21
A FOOLSCAP GIVES US CONFIDENCE

But the strongest reason to do a Foolscap Page is the most obvious. Resistance.

If we're Herman Melville reading over our single-page for *Moby Dick*, we may worry that we can't give our characters sufficient nuance or that we might bore the reader with a too-excessive treatise on the history of "try pots" or the science of rendering sperm whale oil from raw blubber.

But we won't worry that we don't have a story. We won't stew over the ending or freak out that our central character isn't charismatic.

We've got those, and we know it.

A solid Foolscap gives us confidence.

BLACK IRISH JAB #21, "THE FOOLSCAP METHOD"

No law says we must do a Foolscap Page. I've winged it many times, and it has worked.

But is that smart?

Would we set sail for Pago Pago without nautical charts? Would we blast off for Jupiter without coordinates and trajectories?

WEEK FOUR

COVER THE CANVAS

Day 22
THE FIRST DRAFT IS THE HARDEST

You could join the Foreign Legion.

You could cross Antarctica on foot.

Or you could write the first draft of a novel.

Personally, I'd say the first two are easier.

Why?

Because in the first draft (of fiction, of nonfiction, of a screenplay) we are facing the blank page.

In other words, we're confronting Resistance in its purest and most merciless form day after day after day.

BLACK IRISH JAB #14, "COVER THE CANVAS"

People ask sometimes, "When is Resistance strongest?" The answer is easy.

At the start.

First drafts are killers because, even after we've established a beachhead with chapter 1 or Act One, we still have the weight of the whole project before us, day after day after day.

The professional arms herself for this ordeal. She steels herself in advance for the task, knowing it's going to test her like no other arena of the enterprise.

STEVEN PRESSFIELD

Day 23
COVER THE CANVAS

Here's my mantra:

"Cover the canvas."

The most important thing in a first draft (or the first iteration of any enterprise) is to get SOMETHING down on paper that goes from "Chapter 1" to "The End."

Something.

Anything.

Imagine we're Leonardo da Vinci standing before the big, blank canvas on which we will paint *The Last Supper*. What's our priority?

Get paint on every inch of white space—north to south, east to west.

Sketch in the apostles, lay in Jesus, get the supper table down. Don't sweat the details. It doesn't matter if Peter's hair isn't right, or James's left hand has four fingers. We'll fix that later.

BLACK IRISH JAB #14, "COVER THE CANVAS"

There's only one priority in a first draft.

Get the Big Picture down.

Cover the canvas.

Day 24
PERFECTIONISM = RESISTANCE

Have you ever blown an entire writing morning noodling with a single paragraph or, worse, a solitary sentence?

The enemy has outfoxed you.

You have hung up an entire battalion trying to capture an outhouse.

"WRITING WEDNESDAYS," STEVENPRESSFIELD.COM, 12/18/19

Did I forget to say of first drafts …

Momentum is everything.

Day 25
FIRST DRAFTS ARE BLITZKRIEG

In June of 1967, the Israeli armored division under General Israel Tal lay poised on the Egyptian frontier, knowing it was going to have to drive through seven Egyptian divisions to reach its objective, the Suez Canal, on the far side of the Sinai desert. Here is how General Tal concluded his address to his troops:

"Now I'm going to tell you something very severe. *En brera.* 'No alternative.' The battle tomorrow will be life and death. Each man will assault to the end, taking no account of casualties. There will be no retreat. No halt, no hesitation. Only forward assault."

BLACK IRISH JAB #14, "COVER THE CANVAS"

Our creative enterprise, yours and mine, is life and death too. The enemy, Resistance, will employ every ruse, every stratagem, every dirty trick to sap our will and break our momentum. His ally is time. The longer he can drag out the fight, the more likely you and I will be to run out of resources, lose our will, and quit.

Strike fast. Strike hard. Stop for nothing.

Day 26
THE MAGIC OF TK

Matt Quirk is a novelist (*The 500, The Directive, Cold Barrel Zero*). Here in his own words is his secret weapon for getting through a first draft:

Use TK. TK is an editing mark that means "to come" and is equivalent to leaving a blank or brackets in the text.

(It's TK, not TC, because editorial marks are often misspelled intentionally so as not to confuse them with final copy: editors write graf and hed for paragraph and headline).

Can't figure out a character's name? "EvilPoliticianTK."

Need to describe the forest? "He looked out over the SpookyForestDescriptionTK."

TK a whole chapter if you want. Come back...once you've won a few rounds against the existential terror of "Is this whole book going to work or not?" There's no sense filling in the details on scenes that you're going to cut.

BLACK IRISH JAB #14, "COVER THE CANVAS"

The enemy in a first draft, remember, is not faulty dialogue, substandard characterization, or lack of expositional detail. The enemy is Resistance.

Day 27
RESEARCH = RESISTANCE

Let me cite again the movie *Braveheart*.

Wow, was that historically accurate! The filmmakers got the period down perfectly, didn't they? The history, the culture, the weapons, even the spot-on Scottish accents.

Randall Wallace, who wrote *Braveheart*, is a friend. I asked him once how he handled research.

"I never do it. It only slows you down."

What? Wait!

"The most important thing is the story. Get that first. What's the drama about? Who's the hero? Who's the villain? How does it end? Once you get those, you can go back and fill in the research."

"WRITING WEDNESDAYS," STEVENPRESSFIELD.COM, 8/12/2019

Research is for Draft #7 and Draft #11.

Draft #1 is about momentum.

Day 28
THE GOOD NEWS ABOUT FIRST DRAFTS

Yes, there is a positive to first drafts.

A first draft is pure, 190-proof storytelling.

It's fun.

It's crazy.

It's exciting.

A first draft is why you and I became writers in the first place.

We are doing that which only gods and wizards have ever done—we are creating, word-by-word, instant-by-instant, *something that has never existed before.*

BLACK IRISH JAB #14, "COVER THE CANVAS"

First drafts are about you and me and the Muse.

Instinct.

Improv.

Inspiration.

We'll never have this feeling again on this project—the pure, blue-sky rush of casting off the leash and letting the Big Dog run.

WEEK FIVE

"WHERE DO YOU GET YOUR IDEAS?"

Day 29
THE IDEA FOR
THE LEGEND OF BAGGER VANCE

I used to read the *Bhagavad Gita* on airplanes. I figured if the plane went down and I met my Maker, I wanted to be reading something spiritual.

The *Gita* is a mentor-protege story. In it, the troubled warrior Arjuna, on the eve of a great battle, lays down his immortal bow, Gandiva, and refuses to fight. At this point his charioteer steps forward. This charioteer is Krishna, i.e., God in human form. Krishna reads Arjuna the riot act. "You are a warrior! Stand up! Do your duty!"

One day on an airplane I thought, "I'm gonna steal this. I'm gonna use the structure of the *Bhagavad Gita* to write a story about golf."

I didn't know it then, but that loony idea would change my life.

THE AUTHENTIC SWING, **P. 17–18**

A golf novel about spirituality? Who in the world would read such a thing?

Yet less than a year later Robert Redford had signed to direct the movie and Matt Damon, Will Smith, and Charlize Theron had contracted to star in it.

Ideas come to us.

We think we can evaluate them objectively, but we can't. All we can ask of ourselves (and of the universe) is, "Does this idea seize me? Does something about it compel me to do it? Am I willing to put X years of my life into making it happen?"

STEVEN PRESSFIELD

Day 30
THE IDEA FOR *GATES OF FIRE*

I was reading Herodotus's *The Histories* for fun. I came upon this passage:

"Although extraordinary valor was displayed by the entire corps of Spartans and Thespians, yet bravest of all was declared the Spartan Dienekes. It is said that on the eve of the battle, he was told by a native of Trachis [a town near Thermopylae] that the Persian archers were so numerous that when they fired their volleys, the mass of arrows blocked out the sun. Dienekes, however, quite undaunted by this prospect, remarked with a laugh, 'Good. Then we'll have our battle in the shade.'"

At once the twenty-five hundred years between today and 480 BCE melted away. I thought, *I know this man. I can tell his story.*

"THE WARRIOR ARCHETYPE", VIDEO SERIES, 2020

I called the project *Thermopylae* at that point. As with *Bagger Vance*, I thought, *No one is going to be interested in this. A story from twenty-five hundred years ago of a battle nobody's heard of in a place that no one can spell or pronounce? Come on.*

But again, I was seized. I couldn't not do it.

Day 31
THE IDEA FOR *THE VIRTUES OF WAR*

Two sentences came into my mind and refused to go away.

> I have always been a soldier. I have known no
> other life.

I knew instinctively that these were the first two sentences of a book. But what book? About what? And who was the speaker?

I sat with these sentences for months. Then one day I thought, *It's Alexander. Alexander the Great.*

"THE WARRIOR ARCHETYPE", VIDEO SERIES, 2020

Do you believe in the Muse? Do you believe that some source we cannot locate or explain delivers ideas and inspiration to us "out of the blue?"

Where did those first two sentences (above) come from?

The Unconscious? The daimon? The Jungian Self?

Again, I was seized.

Day 32
THE IDEA FOR *THE WAR OF ART*

Friends used to call me up. "Steve, I've got a book in me. Can you help?"

I'd sit up with them until two in the morning, trying to psych them up to overcome their fear, self-doubt, tendency to procrastinate, etc.

In other words, their Resistance.

No one ever listened.

No one ever wrote their book.

But friends still kept coming. "I've got a book in me. Can you help?"

One day I said to myself, "I'm just gonna write all this stuff down in 100 or 150 pages. Then when someone comes to me, I'll hand them the pages and say, 'Here, read this.'"

INTERVIEW WITH OPRAH WINFREY, "SUPER SOUL SUNDAY", 9/20/13

My original title was *The Writer's Life*. I took it to my editor Shawn Coyne, who had just started his own publishing company, Rugged Land Books. "I hate the title," he said. "Lemme think about it and see if I can come up with something better."

Day 33
THE IDEA FOR *LAST OF THE AMAZONS*

I've always hated the institution of the patriarchy. I think it warps and disfigures not only our idea of what a woman is or could be but also what a man is or could be.

One day I was reading Plutarch's *Life of Theseus*—the passage where he describes the attack upon ancient Athens by an army of warrior women.

"For it is impossible that the Amazons should have placed their camp in the very city, and joined battle close by the Pnyx, unless, having first conquered the country around about, they had with impunity advanced to the city. That they encamped there is certain, and may be confirmed by the names that the places thereabout yet retain, and the graves and monuments of those who fell in the battle...For indeed we are also told that [a number] of the Amazons [who] died were buried there in the place that is to this time called Amazoneum."

WRITING SEMINAR, NASHVILLE, 2019

Wow! Could this be true? Could the race of warrior women be not just legend but actual empirical fact?

For a writer of historical fiction, a passage like this one from Plutarch is all it takes. I was off and running.

STEVEN PRESSFIELD

Day 34
THE IDEA FOR *THE LION'S GATE*

I've written about the ancient Spartans and Athenians, about Alexander's Macedonians; I've written about British commandos in World War II. Critics have been kind enough to call me "the finest military writer alive, bar none."

Then one day I find myself thinking about the Six Day War [the Arab-Israeli War of 1967] as the subject for a book.

What a story! A military achievement on a par with Thermopylae or Gettysburg, and it's even deeper because it's about the Jewish people reclaiming their most sacred sites, from which they had been debarred for almost two thousand years.

I said to myself, "Steve, you've written about the wars of others but never about your own people. Don't you think it's about time?"

AN AMERICAN JEW, P. 6

Four months later I was on an El Al jet to Tel Aviv, packing tape recorders, microphones, and as many notebooks as I could stuff into my Samsonite collapsible roller.

Day 35
THE IDEA FOR *A MAN AT ARMS*

Readers ask me sometimes if there's any individual character among all those I've written with whom I identify most. The answer is yes.

It's the solitary mercenary Telamon of Arcadia, who appears in *Tides of War*, re-appears unchanged sixty years later in *The Virtues of War*, and even makes a cameo in *The Profession* twenty years into our contemporary future.

For years I've wanted to write a novel just about him. I can't tell you how many outlines I've started or concepts I've scratched onto yellow foolscap pads. But I never could find the right story or the proper time period.

Then, one day four years ago, I began thinking about another character—a nine-year-old mute girl, in the first century CE, tasked with delivering a certain letter to a certain beleaguered community.

I thought, "This is the story. It's not about just him. It's about him and her."

UNPUBLISHED BLACK IRISH JAB, "ORIGIN STORIES"

One way I think about story trajectories is "Get to 'I love you.'"

That's what we all need. And that's what could save my alter ego, the solitary mercenary Telamon.

WEEK SIX

TWO LEVELS

Day 36
THE UNLIVED LIFE

Most of us have two lives. The life we live, and the unlived life within us. Between the two stands Resistance.

THE WAR OF ART, PREFACE

If life exists on two levels, the Material and the Potential (as I believe it does), where are you and I?

We're part of both levels.

We participate in both.

Our struggle—our "war of art"—is against that invisible, insidious, indefatigable negative force whose sole aim is to block the part of us that resides on the Material plane from reaching out and opening itself up to the part of ourselves that participates in the Plane of the Potential.

STEVEN PRESSFIELD

Day 37
ELIZABETH GILBERT'S TED TALK

"I was in the middle of writing *Eat, Pray, Love*, and I fell into one of those sort of pits of despair...[and] I started to think I should just dump this project. But then I remembered Tom [Waits] talking to the open air [when inspiration for a song hit him while he was driving on the freeway and had no way to record it] and I tried it. So I just lifted my face up from the manuscript and I directed my comments to an empty corner of the room. And I said aloud, 'Listen you, thing, you and I both know that if this book isn't brilliant that is not entirely my fault, right? Because you can see that I am putting everything I have into this. If you want it to be better, you've got to show up and do your part of the deal. But if you don't do that, you know what, the hell with it. I'm going to keep writing anyway because that's my job. And I would please like the record to reflect today that I showed up for my part of the job.'"

ELIZABETH GILBERT TED TALK, NASHVILLE WRITING SEMINAR, 2019

Whatever this "thing" is (see line 7 above), it doesn't reside on this material dimension. Can we find it? Can we call it forth? It sure helps, as Ms. Gilbert testifies, if we work as hard as we can.

Day 38
ALEXANDER AND THE TWO LEVELS

"I felt at home in Egypt. I could happily have been a priest. In truth I am a warrior-priest, who marches where God directs him, in the service of Necessity and Fate. Nor is such a notion vain or self-infatuated. Consider: Persia's time has passed. In the Invisible World, Darius' empire has already fallen. Who am I, except the agent of that end, which already exists in the Other World and at whose birth I assist in this one?"

THE VIRTUES OF WAR, P. 188–189 [HARDBACK]

What fascinates me about the character of Alexander the Great is that he seemed to see the future with such clarity and such intensity as to make it virtually impossible that it would not come true—and that he would be the one to make it do so.

That's you and me at the inception of a creative project.

The book/screenplay/start-up already exists in the Other World.

Your job and mine is to bring it forth in this one.

STEVEN PRESSFIELD

Day 39
AN ANGEL AND A BLADE OF GRASS

It may be pushing the envelope, but if [this higher dimension and the possible beings that inhabit it] take joy in the "creations of time," might they not also nudge us a little to produce them? If that's true, then the image of the Muse whispering inspiration in the artist's ear is quite apt.

The timeless communicating to the timebound.

THE WAR OF ART, P. 117

In Jewish mysticism, the higher dimension is called the *neshama*, the soul.

Indeed, the Kabbalists testify, this loftier sphere is trying to communicate to us, for our benefit, at all times. Above every blade of grass, the sages say, is an angel crying, "Grow! Grow!"

Day 40
"I HAVE DINED ON DREAMS..."

"'I have dined on dreams. Not alone to sustain myself but to set a feast before others. This is how the great identify one another and how the commander of vision leads free men. Ah,' Alcibiades continued, 'but not any dream will do. Only one, and that has a name. It is called Necessity. Necessity is the dream. That which cries out to be born and summons all who call themselves commanders to draw it forth.'"

TIDES OF WAR, P. 313

Tides of War is a historical novel about the twenty-seven-year civil war between Athens and Sparta that spanned the final three decades of the 400s BCE. Its central character is the Athenian general, statesman, and much-maligned political genius Alcibiades.

What amazes me most about Alcibiades's career throughout this long and terrible war was that he, beyond any other figure, compelled events by his actions. Yet for vast intervals he held no office or command. He set the course by the sheer force of his personality. That, and his grasp of what the ancients called "Necessity," by which they meant that unseen force of fate or destiny that drives history.

You and I as writers and artists serve Necessity too. Necessity for us is our own creative destiny, the works we will produce.

Can we discern them?

Do we possess the will and capacity to bring them forth?

Day 41
THE INTERSECTION OF
NECESSITY AND FREE WILL

"What I have tried to do is follow the dictates of Necessity. This is the solitary god I revere and, in my opinion, the only god that exists. Man's predicament is that he dwells at the intersection of Necessity and free will. What distinguishes statesmen, as Themistocles and Pericles, is their gift to perceive Necessity's dictates in advance of others—as Themistocles saw that Athens must become a sea power and Pericles that naval supremacy prefigures empire. That course of individual or nation aligned with Necessity must prove irresistible."

TIDES OF WAR, P. 255–256

This is Alcibiades again (or my fictionalized version of him).

You and I too reside at the intersection of Necessity and free will. Our vocation is Necessity—the works we are called by our unique genius to produce. Free will is that agency that enables us to act.

Our job as artists and as free men and women is to align ourselves with our own Necessity and to summon the resource and resolve to follow the dictates of its call.

Day 42
THE COSMIC RADIO STATION

Did *Rhapsody in Blue* come to Gershwin in the shower? Was J.K. Rowling baking a pie when she first imagined Hogwarts? Or was he at the piano and she at her writing desk?

Like the monk and the mystic, the artist enters a mental space. He becomes a child. She becomes a vessel.

They tune in to the Cosmic Radio Station and listen to whatever song is being broadcast specifically to them.

NOBODY WANTS TO READ YOUR SH*T, P. 183

You and I are cruising across West Texas in our '57 Cadillac Eldorado convertible. We've got the top down and the antenna up. Somewhere out there in the night a radio tower is playing our song.

Can we find it?

Can we still the chatter in our heads and listen hard enough to pick up that signal that was meant for us alone?

WEEK SEVEN

THE ARTIST IN THE TRENCHES

Day 43
ART IS WORK

The most important thing about art is to work. Nothing else matters except sitting down every day and trying.

THE WAR OF ART, P. 108

Are you Michael Jordan? I'm not either. But both of us can work like Michael Jordan.

I have a disagreement with my friend Robert McKee about talent. He thinks talent is the indispensable ingredient in artistic achievement.

I agree, talent is big.

But in the arts, work is bigger.

People tell me now that I'm a talent. But for thirty years they told me I was a bum.

We can all learn.

We can all get better.

Work is everything.

Day 44
A SPARTAN OFFICER

"His was not, I could see now, the heroism of an Achilles. He was not a superman who waded invulnerably into the slaughter, single-handedly slaying the foe by myriads. He was just a man doing a job. A job whose primary attribute was self-restraint and self-composure, not for his own sake, but for those whom he led by his example. A job whose objective could be boiled down to the single understatement, as he did at the Hot Gates on the morning he died, of 'performing the commonplace under uncommonplace conditions.'"

GATES OF FIRE, P. 112–123

When you and I work, we do it on two levels.

One is the soldier in the trenches.

This soldier sweats and bleeds. He charges into the teeth of the foe. He sees only the enemy in front of him and the dirt beneath his feet. He can be crazy, mad, terror-stricken, lost, confused, berserk.

The officer stands above this soldier. She must keep her head, see the big picture, remember the objective, guide and succor and lead by example.

You and I must be both of these when we work.

Day 45
WHAT I KNOW

There's a secret that real writers know and wannabe writers don't, and the secret is this.

It's not the writing part that's hard. What's hard is sitting down to write.

THE WAR OF ART, INTRO PAGES

If you read this statement correctly, it's very, very good news.

It means if you can just make yourself sit down and grind, you can be a writer (or any other kind of artist or entrepreneur).

Day 46
A PROFESSIONAL

Someone once asked Somerset Maugham if he wrote on a schedule or only when struck by inspiration.

"I write only when inspiration strikes," he replied. "Fortunately, it strikes me every morning at nine o'clock sharp."

THE WAR OF ART, **P. 64**

I like to think of the Muse flying overhead every morning, kind of like Santa Claus. She looks down, just to check on you and me. It's nine o'clock. Are we being naughty or nice?

When we say, "Put your ass where your heart wants to be," that's what we mean.

Day 47
THE AMATEUR AND THE PRO

The sign of the amateur is over-glorification of and preoccupation with the mystery. The professional shuts up. She doesn't talk about it. She does her work.

THE WAR OF ART, P. 78

The writer or artist's process is an unlikely amalgam of trench warfare and fly-me-to-the-moon.

The goddess wears combat boots and carries a lunch pail and a thermos.

P.S. She likes it when we do too.

Day 48
IF YOU BUILD IT, SHE WILL COME

The professional masters how, and leaves what and why to the gods. Like Somerset Maugham she doesn't wait for inspiration, she acts in anticipation of its apparition.

THE WAR OF ART, P. 78

All we can do, you and I, is sit down and do our work.

We can't make the Muse show up. We can't compel her. We can't cajole her. We can't bribe her. We can't manipulate her.

But here's the weird thing.

When we carve our baseball diamond out of an Iowa cornfield, the ballplayers show up.

Day 49
"TALENT IS BULLSHIT"

Marty has one other mantra: Talent is bullshit.

"I've seen a million writers with talent. It means nothing. You need guts, you need stick-to-it-iveness. It's work, you gotta work, do the freakin' work. That's why you're gonna make it, son. You work. No one can take that away from you.

"And I'll tell you something else," Marty says to me now over the phone. "Appreciate these days. These days when you're broke and struggling, they're the best days of your life. You're gonna break through, my boy. And when you do, you'll look back on this time and think this is when I was really an artist, when everything was pure and I had nothing but the dream and the work. Enjoy it now. Pay attention. These are the good days. Be grateful for them."

THE KNOWLEDGE, P. 23

Marty in *The Knowledge* was my (fictional) agent, Martin Fabrikant. But I had a real agent at that time, after whom I patterned Marty. His name was Barthold Fles. He represented Kurt Weill, Anaïs Nin, and even Carl Jung. Know what he said about talent?

The exact same thing Marty said.

STEVEN PRESSFIELD

WEEK EIGHT

THE ARTIST IN THE TRENCHES, PART TWO

Day 50
BLUE COLLAR

How many pages have I produced? I don't care. Are they any good? I don't even think about it. All that matters is I've put in my time and hit it with all I've got. All that counts is that, for this day, for this session, I have overcome Resistance.

THE WAR OF ART, INTRO CHAPTER "WHAT I DO"

A screenwriter I admire once told me there are two phases to the writer's work: action and reflection.

In the trenches, what counts is action.

Don't think about it. Write it.

We can always reflect later.

Day 51
THE PROFESSIONAL MINDSET

In one call for recruits, eight hundred applied. The Long Range Desert Group [a British commando unit in WWII] took twelve. But here's what was fascinating to me about the selection process:

The commanders did not want supermen. The ideal volunteer to face the loneliness and isolation of the desert was a working man, preferably a husband and father. Patience was prized more highly than martial valor. The type of individual the LRDG sought was a fellow who could work in close quarters with others under conditions of extreme stress, who did not flee from adversity but rather sought it out and throve on it. The commanders wanted men with a sense of humor. Good mates in a pinch, as they phrased it.

"WRITING WEDNESDAYS," STEVENPRESSFIELD.COM, 3/25/20

Out there alone in the desert, you and I don't have to be Batman or Wonder Woman.

Show up.

Do your job.

Carry on.

Day 52
POWER CONCENTRATES

The Little Prince's planet was so small, he would circumnavigate it at the equator in ten paces. But it had gravity. Its mass generated enough centripetal pull to keep St. Exupery's hero from sailing off into space.

When you and I sit down and write each day (or dance or sing or work on our nonprofit or start-up), we create our own little planet. This planet possesses mass. It has gravity.

Mass attracts mass.

Our planet gets bigger.

Something plus Something equals More Something.

"WRITING WEDNESDAYS," STEVENPRESSFIELD.COM, 11/4/09

Ever wonder why artists and other innovators become so attached to the space in which they work? I can't prove it (and neither can they) but they believe that space becomes physically charged with juju or mojo or whatever you want to call it.

That juju comes from their love and their intensity and their passion.

It gathers. It accrues.

And it draws in more juju.

STEVEN PRESSFIELD

Day 53
VOLUNTEERING FOR HELL

The artist committing himself to his calling has volunteered for hell, whether he knows it or not. He will be dining for the duration on a diet of isolation, rejection, self-doubt, despair, ridicule, contempt, and humiliation.

The artist must be like that Marine. He has to know how to be miserable. He has to love being miserable. Because this is war, baby. And war is hell.

THE WAR OF ART, P. 68

What Marines pride themselves on, among other things, is the ability to embrace the suck. The worse things get, the more at-home Marines feel. The one thing Marines can't stand is for the dirtiest, most dangerous, most miserable assignment to be given to anyone but them.

If you're an artist or an entrepreneur, learn how to spell "Semper Fi." You're one of us.

Day 54
DISTRACTION = RESISTANCE

The amateur tweets. The pro works.

TURNING PRO, P. 93

We can say distraction is Resistance.

But it's not really distraction.

It's self-distraction.

We allow ourselves to follow that Facebook thread or go down that rabbit hole or say yes when we know we should say no.

Nobody is doing this to us.

We're doing it to ourselves.

STEVEN PRESSFIELD

Day 55
WHEN IN DOUBT, IT'S RESISTANCE

Hi, Tiana …

Indeed, I do remember you and our eggs benny with Jeff. Congrats on your new career and opportunities going forward. To answer your question:

I have an axiom I use for myself when I'm stuck between, "Is it Resistance or is it Intuition?"

When in doubt, it's Resistance.

What I mean is Resistance is so diabolical and so clever at camouflaging itself as something "rational" or "pragmatic," that to err on the side of identifying it as Resistance is a pretty good bet.

FROM AN E-MAIL EXCHANGE WITH A YOUNG ENTREPRENEUR, 5/20/20

Nothing is certain in life, but one phenomenon is close. If your fevered brain is presenting you with some reason/excuse/rationalization why you should *not* undertake some project or challenge or opportunity that you feel in your gut is the right thing to do…

It ain't legit.

It's Resistance.

Day 56
IT AIN'T ME, BABE

Have you seen archival footage of the young John Lennon or Bob Dylan, when some reporter tries to ask them about their personal selves? The boys deflect these queries with withering sarcasm. Why? Because Lennon and Dylan know that the part of them that writes the songs is not "them," not the personal self that is of such surpassing fascination to their boneheaded interrogators.

Lennon and Dylan also know that the part of themselves that does the writing is too sacred, too precious, too fragile to be dumbed down into sound bites for the titillation of would-be idolaters (who are themselves caught up in their own Resistance). So they put them on and blow them off.

THE WAR OF ART, P. 44

Ego is the enemy, writes Ryan Holiday in his 2016 book of the same title. Ryan is talking about spiritual and ethical evolution, about self-realization. But ego is the enemy of the artist too.

As long as you and I are centered in the "I" of our minds, the good stuff ain't gonna come.

The artist's job is to quiet this little "I" and get to the "Big I" beyond it.

WEEK NINE

WHO ARE YOU?

Day 57
WHICH "I" AM I?

When we call ourselves "I," which "I" do we mean?

There's the first "I"—our ego, our conscious self, our reasoning intellect.

But if we go to yoga class or sit down to meditate, we come immediately upon a second "I." This "I" watches us as we enter downward dog or try to calm the mindless chatter between our ears. This "I" is a witness. It's somewhere "behind" or "above" the first "I."

There's a third "I" that can witness us witnessing ourselves.

Not to mention a fourth that stands in for us in our dreams.

There's a fifth "I" as well. That's the one who writes our books, paints our paintings, starts our start-ups.

The fifth "I" operates independently of the first four.

That's the "I" I'm interested in.

"WRITING WEDNESDAYS," STEVENPRESSFIELD.COM, 6/10/20

People ask me sometimes, "Don't you get lonely being in a room by yourself all day?"

No.

I'm not lonely because I'm with this other "me," who is me and not-me at the same time and whom I have spent my entire life trying to find, to prove myself worthy of, and to labor in collaboration with.

Day 58
AUTHENTIC SWING = AUTHENTIC SELF

"I believe that each of us possesses, inside ourselves," Bagger Vance began, "one true Authentic Swing that is ours alone. It is folly to try to teach us another, or to mold us to some ideal version of the perfect swing. Each player possesses only that one swing that he was born with, that swing which existed within him before he ever picked up a club. Like the Statue of David, our Authentic Swing already exists, concealed within the stone, so to speak."

Keeler broke in with excitement. "Then our task as golfers, according to this line of thought..."

"...is simply to chip away all that is inauthentic, allowing our Authentic Swing to emerge in its purity."

THE LEGEND OF BAGGER VANCE, P. 68 [HARDBACK]

You and I are not born as *tabula rasa*—blank slates. We are not free to become "anyone we want to be."

Rather, our task is to become who we already are.

Day 59
NOBODY KNOWS NOTHING

This is my twenty-third book. Looking back, here's the Big Takeaway:

I never had any idea, before I wrote a book, that I was going to write it. The book always came out of nowhere and always took me by surprise.

Let me express this a different way:

No matter what a writer or artist may tell you, they have no clue what they're doing before they do it—and, for the most part, while they're doing it.

Or another way:

Everything we produce as artists comes from a source beyond our conscious awareness.

THE ARTIST'S JOURNEY, P. 57

Who is this mysterious "I"—the one who dances our dance, sings our song, writes our poetry?

Is it inside us or outside?

How can we reach her?

How can we make her appear?

Day 60
A RECURRING DREAM

Jackson Browne once said that he writes to find out what he thinks. (Wait, it was Joan Didion who said that…no, Stephen King said it too.)

I do the same, and you do too, whether you realize it or not.

The key pronoun here is "you."

Who is this "you"?

1. "You," meaning the writer of your books, is not you. Not the "you" you think of as yourself.

2. This "secret you" is smarter than you are. A lot smarter. This "you" is the real you.

THE ARTIST'S JOURNEY, P. 37–38

I have a recurring dream. A good dream.

I'm in my house when I realize I'm in a room I didn't know I had. Sometimes that room is a cute little cubby. Other times it's a vast, Vegas-style party space with bands playing and people dancing.

The dream is telling me that there are parts of myself I'm not aware of.

That's what the idea for a new book feels like. Each one surprises me. Each comes from a place I never knew existed.

I say every time, "Where the hell did *that* come from?"

Day 61
WHERE DO BOOKS/MOVIES/SONGS COME FROM?

My long-held belief is that an artist's identity is revealed by the works he or she produces.

Writers do not write to express themselves. They write to discover themselves.

But who is this "self" they seek to discover?

It is that deeper, wiser you—that waterproof, bulletproof, self-propelled, self-contained "you."

Every work we produce as artists comes from that "you."

Our first "you" is nothing but the vehicle that contains (and initially conceals) this real you.

THE ARTIST'S JOURNEY, P. 59

The corollary to this idea—that the artist's identity is revealed by the works she produces—is equally fascinating.

The artist has no idea what works she will produce.

It's pointless, in my opinion, to produce a five-year plan or to project ourselves in imagination into the future. As my friend David Leddick says, "You meet somebody and you wind up living in another country, speaking another language."

For the artist, that "somebody" is herself.

STEVEN PRESSFIELD

Day 62
THE ARTIST BELIEVES IN
A DIFFERENT REALITY

Did you ever see the Meg Ryan-Nicholas Cage movie, *City of Angels*? In the film (screenplay by Dana Stevens), human characters go about their lives oblivious of the cohort of angels—male and female, all handsome, all dressed in stylish duster-length coats—who attend upon them and are present beside them, often standing invisibly directly at their shoulders.

That's my world.

That's what I see.

Everything I do is based upon that reality.

THE ARTIST'S JOURNEY, P. 108

The artist's universe is constituted of two dimensions—the material world, in which we dwell in "real life"…and the sphere of potentiality.

The first is What Is.

The second is What Will (or Can) Be.

The artist eats, breathes, and loves in the material world, but his true being exists in the higher realm.

Day 63
THE ARTIST'S SKILL

What exactly does an artist do? The writer, the dancer, the film-maker...what, precisely, does their work consist of?

They shuttle from Level #1 to Level #2 and back again.

Twyla Tharp in her dance studio, Quentin Tarantino on his movie set, Bob Dylan in the recording studio. They perform this simple but miraculous act a thousand, ten thousand times a day.

They enter the Second World and come back to the First with something that had never existed in the First World before.

A machine can't do that. AI can't do that. In all of Creation, only two creatures can do that.

Gods.

And you and me.

THE ARTIST'S JOURNEY, P. 68

Why are artists often so surprisingly humble? Because they know, despite the seeming magic they produce, (and the effect it has upon their audience or their readers) that they are not the source. They are only the vessel, the pipeline.

STEVEN PRESSFIELD

WEEK TEN

A BODY OF WORK, PART ONE

Day 64
YOUR AGENT WANTS A SECOND BOOK

As you read this, are you at some point—beginning, middle, or end—in the writing of your first book?

Start thinking about Book #2.

I'm serious.

Professional athletes think in terms of careers, as do dancers and filmmakers and restaurateurs and entrepreneurs.

You and I need to too.

"WRITING WEDNESDAYS," STEVENPRESSFIELD.COM, 11/13/19

Can you picture a shelf of books? Your books.

Ten of 'em.

Fifteen.

Twenty.

Can you imagine not just one title but an actual body of work?

Day 65
A DUDE FROM NEW JERSEY

Consider this (slightly abridged) body of work:

Greetings from Asbury Park, N.J.
The Wild, the Innocent & the E Street Shuffle
Born to Run
Darkness on the Edge of Town
The River
Nebraska
Born in the USA
Tunnel of Love
The Ghost of Tom Joad
Wrecking Ball
High Hopes
Springsteen on Broadway

THE ARTIST'S JOURNEY, P. 29

I love to consider the work of an artist I admire *as a totality*.

See the theme in there? See the unity? See the evolution over time?

No one else who has ever lived or ever will live could have produced this body of work.

It is totally Springsteenian. It's his heart. His soul.

It's him.

ANOTHER DUDE FROM NEW JERSEY

Now consider this body of work:

Goodbye, Columbus
Portnoy's Complaint
My Life as a Man
The Professor of Desire
Zuckerman Unbound
The Anatomy Lesson
The Counterlife
Sabbath's Theater
American Pastoral
The Human Stain
The Plot Against America
Indignation

Philip Roth passed on in 2018, so we know the above (slightly abridged) body of work is complete.

WRITING SEMINAR, NASHVILLE, 2019

Could any other soul have written these books?

Not Saul Bellow. Not Woody Allen. Not Milton or Dante or Shakespeare himself. These works are collectively Roth's statement, his art, his expression of the unique being and point of view that was his and his alone.

Day 67
JONI

Let's rack up a third artist's (again slightly abridged) body of work:

Clouds
Both Sides Now
Ladies of the Canyon
Blue
For the Roses
Court and Spark
The Hissing of Summer Lawns
Hejira
Don Juan's Reckless Daughter
Wild Things Run Fast
Chalk Mark in a Rain Storm
Night Ride Home
Turbulent Indigo

WRITING SEMINAR, NASHVILLE, 2019

Again we see a theme, a unique perspective, an evolution over time.
We might remark as well (of all three artists) that we see a destiny.
There's something almost preordained about these three artists' bodies of work, isn't there?
It's as if they had no choice.

Day 68
WHO ARE YOU, PART TWO

If you'll forgive me, let me set my own body of work before us for consideration:

> *The Legend of Bagger Vance*
> *Gates of Fire*
> *Tides of War*
> *Last of the Amazons*
> *The War of Art*
> *The Afghan Campaign*
> *Turning Pro*
> *The Lion's Gate*
> *The Artist's Journey*
> *A Man at Arms*
> *Put Your Ass Where Your Heart Wants To Be*
> *Govt Cheese: A Memoir*

I'll say it again. I never had any idea, before I wrote a book, that I was going to write it. The book always came out of nowhere and always took me by surprise.

WRITING SEMINAR, NASHVILLE, 2019

An "I" wrote these. That "I" is not the "I" I consider "myself." But that "I" is me. It's the real me.

STEVEN PRESSFIELD

Day 69
A BODY OF WORK
EXISTS IN AND OF ITSELF

I believe that Bruce Springsteen's albums existed before he ever picked up a guitar.

As did Bob Dylan's and Joni Mitchell's and George Gershwin's.

They existed, I believe, on another plane of reality. Maybe not note for note, maybe not line for line. But in some form that was recognizably Dylanesque or Mitchell-like or Gershwin-close.

Dylan and Joni and Gershwin tuned themselves to the Cosmic Radio Station and heard the music that was for them alone to bring forth.

"WRITING WEDNESDAYS," STEVENPRESSFIELD.COM, 6/17/20

Do you believe me? Then believe this.

You too have a body of work.

It exists inside you...and has existed from the moment you were born and possibly even before that.

Your body of work, like Bruce's or Joni's or Philip Roth's, is unique to you. No other individual, living or dead, can produce or could have produced it.

It is yours alone, and it is real.

Day 70
A BODY OF WORK EXERTS A PRESSURE

This body of work in potential exerts a powerful, irresistible pressure. It seeks to be brought into realization in the material world.

Like a biological clock or the need to live out one's hero's journey, this unborn entity aches and agitates to be brought into physical existence.

We can ignore this call if we choose.

We can blow it off or pretend it doesn't exist (or pour ourselves into parallel or "shadow" careers).

But the pressure does not go away.

Some might say it intensifies over time.

WRITING SEMINAR, NASHVILLE, 2019

What happens if we don't live out this body of work?

I'm not a doctor, but my supposition is it (the energy of these works-in-potential) diverts itself into other channels of our psyche, producing—pick your poison—depression, anxiety, anger, despair, etc. and manifesting itself in such vices as drug abuse, alcoholism, weight gain or loss, domestic abuse, and so forth, all the familiar maladies of contemporary life.

WEEK ELEVEN

SELF-TALK AND SELF-COMMAND

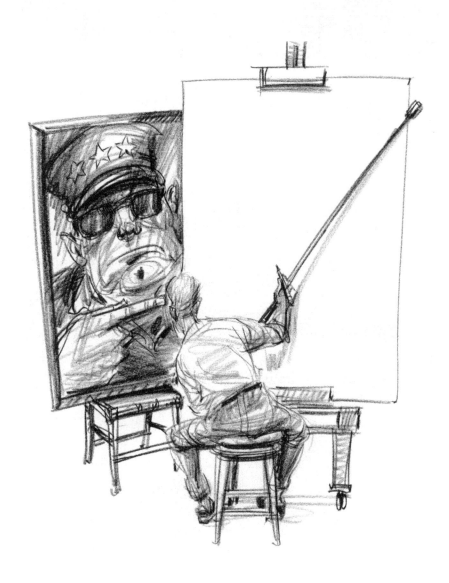

Day 71
CAN WE COMMAND OURSELVES?

"You are the commanders. Your men will look to you and act as you do. Let no officer keep to himself or his brother officers, rather circulate daylong among his men. Let them see you and see you unafraid. Where there is work to do, turn your hand to it first; the men will follow. If there is no work, make it up, for when soldiers have time to talk, their talk turns to fear. Action, on the other hand, produces the appetite for more action."

KING LEONIDAS IN *GATES OF FIRE*, P. 226 [HARDBACK]

If I keep returning to the King archetype, it's because I believe we as writers and artists must activate this avatar within ourselves.

Yes, the favor of the Muse is critical. We cannot work without that flow from heaven. But we need a presence of self-command here on Earth, on the ground, in the trenches.

We must be our own commanders, our own archetypes of self-command.

Day 72
MY YEAR OF TURNING PRO

I was thirty-one. I had saved up $2,700 and moved from New York to a little town in Northern California. I rented a house behind another house for $105 a month. I had my old Chevy van, my Smith-Corona typewriter, and my cat, Mo.

I didn't talk to anybody during my year of turning pro. I didn't hang out. I just worked. I had a book in mind and I had decided I would finish it or kill myself. I could not run away again, or let people down again, or let myself down again. This was it, do or die.

TURNING PRO, P. 42

I did finish the book. I didn't kill myself. But I couldn't find a buyer for it, or for the one after it. It would be another twenty-one years before a real-life publisher accepted something I had written and brought it out as a finished book.

In the end, the wait didn't matter. That year gave me, for the first time in my life, an uninterrupted stretch of month after month that was mine alone, when I was truly productive, truly facing my demons, and truly working my shit.

That year has stuck with me.

Day 73
AN ACTOR SOMETIMES

"In combat there is no time for grief. A commander must act. He must project decisiveness and certainty. No matter how grim the situation, he must act as if it is under control. If your soldiers read fear on your face or discern irresolution in your posture, you have failed them.

"The combat commander must be an actor sometimes. This is war. You must use everything. Everything."

MAJOR UZI EILAM FROM *THE LION'S GATE*, P. 279–280 [PAPERBACK]

Sometimes we as artists and entrepreneurs must be actors, not only for others but also for ourselves.

Can we convince ourselves that we're not afraid? That we can pull off the crazy, unprecedented enterprise that we've just embarked on?

STEVEN PRESSFIELD

Day 74
YOUR MIND CHANGES
WHEN YOU TURN PRO

Turning pro is like kicking a drug habit or stopping drinking. It's a decision, a decision to which we must re-commit every day.

Each day, the professional understands, she will wake up to the same demons, the same Resistance, the same self-sabotage, the same tendencies to shadow activities and amateurism that she has always faced.

The difference is that now she will not yield to these temptations.

She will have mastered them, and she will continue to master them.

TURNING PRO, P. 74

Self-talk implies a conversation—a speaker and a listener.

You and I are the speaker and the listener.

We are she who commands and she who follows that command.

When we turn pro, the self who speaks, speaks with authority. And the self who listens hears and willingly obeys.

Day 75
"THE REAL WAR IS INSIDE MY HEAD"

"For every man under my responsibility, I see in my mind's eye his mother and father, his girlfriend or wife, his children, even if he has none yet. All will suffer if he dies. Such a weight makes concerns such as personal fear, loss, even one's own death seem trivial.

"War for the commander is not like war for the individual soldier. What is going on in external reality is for me only context. The real war is inside my head.

"In my head I must overlook nothing, forget nothing, fail to act on no warning or intuition. I am lucky. My position of responsibility denies me the luxury of doubt or hesitation or fear."

ISRAELI ARMY CAPTAIN ORI ORR, FROM *THE LION'S GATE*, P. 344 [PAPERBACK]

For the artist or the entrepreneur, leadership implies a dimension beyond that which we associate with soldiers or statesmen or chairpersons of corporations.

It implies self-leadership.

The writer, the painter, the filmmaker is alone. She must lead not platoons or battalions but herself. When she cries, "Follow me!" and charges into the teeth of the enemy, she herself must follow.

Making yourself a corporation (or just thinking of yourself in that way) reinforces the idea of professionalism because it separates the artist-doing-the-work from the will-and-consciousness running the show. Sometimes, as Joe Blow myself, I'm too meek and mild-mannered to go out and sell my stuff. But as Joe Blow Inc. I can pimp the hell out of myself.

I'm not me anymore.

I'm Me, Inc.

I'm a pro.

THE WAR OF ART, P. 97–98

Is it crazy to talk to ourselves or to create mind-games like incorporating ourselves so we can outfox our own Resistance and tendency to self-sabotage?

Not to me it isn't.

My Resistance is monumental.

I'll use every trick in the book to overcome it.

Day 77
NIGHT FIGHTING IN JERUSALEM

"In battle soldiers hide. Officers hide. They are afraid. They don't want to be killed. Someone has ordered them to capture a certain house. But they have seen six of their friends enter that house and none has come out. So they make themselves invisible.

"This is how an advance stalls. An officer is not willingly acting the coward. He is trying to gather himself for a minute, to collect his men and his thoughts. But sixty seconds becomes twenty minutes and pretty soon two hours have passed and that house is still killing your men.

"As commander, you have to go there. You must find the officer on-site. When he sees you, he will act. If he cannot, you must replace him. Right then."

MAJOR UZI EILAM FROM *THE LION'S GATE*, P. 281 [PAPERBACK]

You—the artist, the writer, the filmmaker—must be as ruthless with yourself as a commander in battle is with the officers and men under his direction.

The fight is to the finish.

Either you will win or the enemy will.

STEVEN PRESSFIELD

WEEK TWELVE

THE INCITING INCIDENT

Day 78

EVERY FIRST ACT MUST
HAVE AN INCITING INCIDENT

I took Robert McKee's class. It was called Screenplay Structure then. The class was full of other aspiring screenwriters as well as actors and actresses, studio execs and development guys and gals. We were all desperate to find out what made a movie work.

McKee delivered.

About an hour into Friday evening's class, he introduced the concept of the Inciting Incident. The Inciting Incident is the event that makes the story start. It had never occurred to me that a story needed to start. I thought it started all by itself.

And I certainly had never realized that the writer had to consciously craft that specific moment when the story starts.

NOBODY WANTS TO READ YOUR SH*T, P. 72

Like every other writer in Tinseltown, I had a sheaf of my own (unsold) scripts in the trunk of my car. I remember dashing out to the parking lot as soon as McKee's seminar ended and thumbing frantically through pages.

Did I have any inciting incidents?

Was their absence the reason nobody wanted to buy my stuff?

Day 79
THE INCITING INCIDENT IN *HAMLET*

GHOST OF HAMLET'S FATHER
'Tis given out that, sleeping in my orchard, a
serpent stung me; so that the whole ear of
Denmark is by a forged process of my death
rankly abused; but know, thou noble youth,
the serpent that did sting thy father's life now
wears his crown.

HAMLET
O my prophetic soul! My uncle!

This (and the remainder of the ghost's speech, which concludes with "Remember me!") is the inciting incident of *Hamlet*.

"WRITING WEDNESDAYS," STEVENPRESSFIELD.COM, 8/10/16

Everything in the play until this moment has been "setup." Only now, with this revelation, does the story really begin.

Note especially that in this moment Hamlet *acquires his intention*—to expose his uncle's treachery, to revenge his father's murder, and to set things right within the royal court of Denmark.

This drive will carry him (and us in the audience) through to the final bloody climax.

Day 80
THE DIFFERENCE BETWEEN
SETUP AND INCITING INCIDENT

Here's Blake Snyder on the subject of setup from *Save the Cat!* (one of my favorite books on storytelling):

"[The setup] is where we see the world as it is before the adventure starts. It is a full-fledged documentation of the hero's world labeled 'before.' If the events that follow did not occur, it would pretty much stay this way. But there is a sense in the setup that a storm's about to hit, because for things to stay as they are…is death. Things *must* change."

"WRITING WEDNESDAYS," STEVENPRESSFIELD.COM 8/10/16

It's a helpful exercise to study books or movies you love, asking yourself, "When does the setup end and the inciting incident come in?"

How soon in *Ad Astra* does Brad Pitt get drafted to go into space to find his renegade father, Tommy Lee Jones?

When, in Homer's *Iliad*, do we learn that Achilles in pride and outrage will withdraw from the fighting?

Day 81

IN THE INCITING INCIDENT, THE HERO ACQUIRES HIS INTENTION

The Bourne Identity begins with Jason Bourne (Matt Damon) floating unconscious in the Mediterranean, at night, a serious distance offshore. The crew of a fishing boat spots him and hauls him aboard. (So far, this is all setup.)

Examining Bourne's unconscious form, the fishermen discover two bullets lodged in the Kevlar vest/wetsuit he is wearing. They also discover a tiny pellet-like device implanted in Bourne's flesh. When they extract this doohickey, they see that it projects the name of a Swiss bank and a number that apparently belongs to a no-doubt-secret account.

Bourne comes to with a violent start and furiously attacks the crewman who has just saved his life. It takes long moments before he can be calmed down and made to realize that he's safe. He is not among enemies.

"Who are you?" asks the crewman.

"I don't know," replies Jason.

BLACK IRISH JAB #10, "HOW DOES A STORY START?"

See how Jason Bourne in this instant acquires the intention that will carry him through the whole rest of the movie—to discover who he is, to find out who tried to kill him, and to get to the bottom of whatever crazy stuff is going on in his crazy life?

Day 82
DOES NONFICTION
NEED AN INCITING INCIDENT?

Have you watched Elizabeth Gilbert's twenty-plus-million-view TED talk, "Your Elusive Creative Genius"?

"[Something] peculiar has happened recently in my life…I wrote this book, this memoir called *Eat, Pray, Love*, which…became this big, mega-sensation, international bestseller thing. The result of which is that everywhere I go now, people treat me like I'm doomed. Seriously—doomed, doomed! Like, they come up to me now, all worried, and they say, 'Aren't you afraid you're never going to be able to top that? Aren't you afraid you're going to keep writing for your whole life and you're never again going to create a book that anybody in the world cares about at all, ever again?'"

"WRITING WEDNESDAYS," STEVENPRESSFIELD.COM, 6/24/20

See the inciting incident? It's the moment when "people" (and by extension Elizabeth herself) start to fear for the writer's future, seeking to follow up her huge bestselling hit. In this moment Ms. Gilbert acquires her intention—to find some mindset that either obviates or overcomes this terror. (Full disclosure—she does.) We as nonfiction writers need an inciting incident just as much as fiction writers do.

Day 83
THE CLIMAX IS EMBEDDED IN
THE INCITING INCIDENT

Apollo Creed picks Rocky Balboa out of the book of fighters and says, "I'm gonna give this chump a shot at the title." That's the Inciting Incident of *Rocky*.

How do we know? Because as soon as we see it, we know that the climax of the movie will be Apollo and Rocky slugging it out for the heavyweight championship of the world.

In *Taken*, sex traffickers kidnap Liam Neeson's daughter. Liam manages to get on the phone with these villains. He tells them to let her go or else. "I have a very specific set of skills and I'm going to use them to hunt you down and kill you." The Bad Guys taunt him with "Good luck" and hang up.

NOBODY WANTS TO READ YOUR SH*T, P. 75

Anticipation of experiencing the climax pulls us, the audience, through both movies. We can't wait to see if Rocky can somehow hang in with the champ...or what mayhem Liam Neeson will unleash when he catches up with the dastardly kidnappers of his daughter.

If your Climax is not embedded in your Inciting Incident, you don't have an Inciting Incident.

Day 84
INCITING INCIDENT = "THE CALL"

The Call and the Inciting Incident are identical. Both serve the same narrative purpose. They hook the reader and they get the story started. Here's Christopher Vogler from *The Writer's Journey:*

"[In the moment of 'the Call'], the hero is presented with a problem, challenge, or adventure to undertake. Once presented with a Call of Adventure, she can no longer remain indefinitely in the comfort of the Ordinary World.

"In *Star Wars*, the Call to Adventure is Princess Leia's desperate holographic message to wise old Obi-Wan Kenobi, who asks Luke to join in the quest. In revenge plots, the Call to Adventure is often a wrong, which must be set right. In romantic comedies, [it's] the first encounter with the special but annoying someone the hero or heroine will be pursuing and sparring with."

"WRITING WEDNESDAYS," STEVENPRESSFIELD.COM, 9/7/16

We'll study the hero's journey in great detail as the days of this book unfold. Suffice it to say for the moment that every story, from the Bible to *South Park*, starts with an inciting incident that is the equivalent of "the Call" and proceeds into a "Journey" undertaken by a "Hero."

WEEK THIRTEEN

THREE-ACT STRUCTURE

Day 85
THREE-ACT STRUCTURE

In Los Angeles I starved for about five years. I wrote nine screenplays on spec. Each one took about six months. I couldn't sell any of them.

But I learned what a screenplay is.

A movie script is composed of three acts. Act One: page 1 to about page 25. Act Two: page 25 to about page 75–85. Act Three: to the finish, page 105–120.

When someone first told me this (no doubt another fledgling writer) I immediately thought, "What formulaic bullshit! I'm not gonna be a slave to that!"

Wrong.

If there is a single principle that is indispensable to structuring any kind of dramatic or comic narrative (including nonfiction), it is this:

Break the piece into three parts—beginning, middle, and end.

NOBODY WANTS TO READ YOUR SH*T, P. 57

Also known as Hook, Build, and Payoff. More on this to come.

Day 86
THE BOSS DEMONSTRATES THREE-ACT STRUCTURE

ACT ONE
I met her in a Kingstown bar.
We fell in love. I knew it had to end.

ACT TWO
We took what we had
And we ripped it apart.

ACT THREE
Now here I am, down in Kingstown again.

NOBODY WANTS TO READ YOUR SH*T, P. 59

The concept behind three-act structure is often defined as Hook, Build, Payoff.

Hook the audience with Act One. Build suspense and raise the stakes through Act Two. Then pay it all off emotionally and thematically in the climax, in Act Three.

If there is a more concise example of this than the verses above from Bruce Springsteen's "Hungry Heart," I've never seen it.

Day 87
MOBY DICK IN THREE ACTS

ACT ONE
Ahab and crew of *Pequod* set out in pursuit of Moby Dick.

ACT TWO
Ahab, crew, and *Pequod* hunt Moby Dick around the world.

ACT THREE
Ahab, crew, and *Pequod* catch Moby Dick, duel him to the death.

WRITING SEMINAR, NASHVILLE, 2019

Even a five-hundred-plus page book can be boiled down to Beginning, Middle, and End.

Hook, Build, Payoff.

But books and movies are not the only works that follow this paradigm. Dance, music, sculpture, photography, painting, even the design of restaurants and museums, of buildings and entire cities practices this one-two-three progression.

Day 88
THE VIETNAM VETERANS' MEMORIAL
IN THREE ACTS

ACT ONE

A polished black marble wall, set within the National Mall in Washington DC, with the names of the fallen in chronological order of the dates of their deaths.

ACT TWO

The wall is set below the level of the ground in a "V" extending from a shallow end to a deep end. Visitors descend to view the wall, passing at close range along its length.

ACT THREE

No barrier prevents the visitors from touching the names of the memorialized or from leaving tokens of love or honor at the base of the wall.

DO THE WORK, P. 24

See how the protagonist—the visitor to the Vietnam Memorial—is channeled by her physical passage into experiencing a story?

From her approach to the Wall (Act One) through her descent and transit past the names of the fallen (Act Two) to her arrival at the name of the loved one she has lost (Act Three, climax), she is forced by the artist Maya Lin's concept of the memorial to participate in a drama that progresses emotionally from a Hook to a Build to a Payoff.

Day 89
THE LAST SUPPER IN THREE ACTS

ACT ONE

Supper table stretching horizontally across the width of the canvas.

ACT TWO

Jesus standing in the center, apostles arrayed in various postures right and left.

ACT THREE

Perspective and background tailing off behind.

***DO THE WORK*, P. 23**

Viewing *The Last Supper*, our vision is struck first by the wide horizontal presence of the table (Act One), which dominates the work and defines it as an opus of scale.

Next, the eye tracks to (Act Two) the "cast" with its "star" and "supporting players." Remember too that the artist, Leonardo da Vinci, knew that every observer would bring with him or her a knowledge of the occasion of the Last Supper and the apotheosis that would unfold inevitably upon the morrow.

Finally (Act Three) our eye takes in the background extending into infinity in perfectly realized perspective. In other words, this narrative of the crucifixion of Jesus of Nazareth would radiate perpetually into the wider world.

Day 90
"POSITIVELY FOURTH STREET"
IN THREE ACTS

ACT ONE

"You got a lotta nerve to say you are my friend ..."

ACT TWO

"... when you know as well as me you'd rather see me paralyzed."

ACT THREE

"... you'd know what a drag it is to see you."

DO THE WORK, P. 24

Act One of this classic Bob Dylan song establishes hero (the singer), villain (whomever he's addressing in the lyrics of the song), theme (the hypocrisy of friendship among hipster street people), and inciting incident (some off-camera gesture of false camaraderie on the part of the singer's friend).

Act Two moves through progressive ratchetings-up of the stakes between singer and friend, culminating in the articulation of the down-and-dirty truth.

Act Three is the payoff. The statement by the singer that he sees through the protestations of his false friend, culminating in the final contemptuous screw-you kiss-off.

Day 91
THE DAVID LEAN RULE

David Lean was the master film director of *Lawrence of Arabia, Doctor Zhivago, The Bridge on the River Kwai* and many others. He had a principle that applies beautifully not just to movies but to novels and other long-form fiction and nonfiction.

Lean said, "Every work can be divided into between eight and twelve major sequences."

This is an alternative to the idea of Three Act Structure.

Watch *Lawrence of Arabia* carefully. You'll see that Lean followed his own rule. The movie is constituted of focused, self-contained sequences, each of which may contain ten, fifteen, twenty scenes. Each sequence is like a movie within a movie, and each sequence sets the stage for the sequences that follow.

Because of this, the story unspools with an epic grandeur. It feels stately, majestic, monumental.

NOBODY WANTS TO READ YOUR SH*T, P. 60–61

Sometimes a work is too long (or consumed over too great a stretch of time) to consist of only three acts. It needs five or six. Or, as David Lean says, eight to twelve.

But whatever the number of acts, there is always a Hook, always a Build, and always a Payoff.

STEVEN PRESSFIELD

WEEK FOURTEEN

HEEDING THE CALL

Day 92
ACT ONE CURTAIN

In the theater, Act One ends and the curtain comes down. The audience gets it. One part of the story has concluded and another is about to begin.

Writers for the screen and TV produce the same effect with an imaginary curtain that the audience feels, even if the story doesn't stop to memorialize this.

Rocky agrees to fight the champ. Curtain comes down.

Captain Miller's squad is assigned to find Private Ryan. Curtain comes down.

Luke Skywalker heads to Mos Eisley spaceport with Obi-Wan Kenobi to seek a ship to go save Princess Leia. Curtain comes down.

UNPUBLISHED BLACK IRISH JAB, "ACT ONE CURTAIN"

The idea of an invisible Act One Curtain is a tremendously powerful tool in structuring a story, not just for our readers but for ourselves.

You and I as novelists should consider using it.

Day 93
IDENTIFYING OUR ACT ONE CURTAIN

In story meetings in Hollywood, the question will be asked directly: "What's our Act One Curtain?"

What the producer or financier (or actor or story editor or development person) means is, "What is the moment when our hero passes out of the Ordinary World and enters the Extraordinary World?"

Dorothy and Toto are swept away from Kansas by a cyclone.

Anna Karenina falls in love with Count Vronsky.

Addie Loggins sets out for St. Joe, Missouri, with Moses Pray.

UNPUBLISHED BLACK IRISH JAB, "ACT ONE CURTAIN"

In laying out my own stories, I ask myself the same question: "What exact moment does my hero leave the Ordinary World and enter the Extraordinary World?"

Do I have such a moment?

Is it unclear? Is it derivative? Is it lame?

Day 94
HEEDING THE CALL

"Severus [the Roman garrison commander of Jerusalem] produced a leather pouch. He tossed it onto the joinery table between himself and the man-at-arms.

"'Note, my friends, that I proffer to this soldier-for-hire no description of the task I wish him to perform. I display only such reward as its successful completion commands. Why? Because our brother-in-arms here, who is too good to call himself a Roman and too proud to accept citizenship beneath our standard, regards all chores of war as equally worthy or worthless. He asks one thing only: 'How much does it pay?'"

"'I accept,' said Telamon. "'What's the job?'"

A MAN AT ARMS, P. 31–32 [HARDBACK]

Huck Finn heeds the call when he takes off on a raft down the Mississippi with his friend, the runaway slave Jim. Rocky heeds it when he accepts the fight promoter's offer to take on the champ. Wonder Woman heeds the call when she departs the island of Themiscyra with pilot Steve Trevor to take on the evil god Ares in WWI.

If our story hasn't got a call (and if our hero doesn't heed it), we haven't got a story.

Day 95
REFUSAL OF THE CALL

When Rocky first gets offered the chance to fight the champ, he turns it down.

Odysseus pretends to be mad, seeking to evade the draft that will take him to Troy.

Even Luke Skywalker, confronted with the hologram call for help from Princess Leia, insists at first that he can't leave his responsibilities on Uncle Owen and Aunt Varoo's evaporator farm.

The notion that the hero's first response to the Call is to turn it down is, according to Joseph Campbell, common to the preponderance of journey myths across all cultures throughout history.

WRITING SEMINAR, NASHVILLE, 2019

I have a different term for this phenomenon.

Resistance.

Any time we (or the heroes in our stories) find ourselves poised at the threshold of adventure, of a leap of faith into the unknown, it's only natural for us to freak out and want to run the other way.

The voice of our own Resistance is overwhelming us.

Some of us have spent years in the state of "refusal of the call."

My own term was seven years, from age twenty-four to thirty-one.

I put 270,000 miles on my ancient Chevy van running away from the call.

(Of course, in those days I had never heard of "the call" or "the hero's journey." The concept of Resistance was totally unknown to me.)

WRITING SEMINAR, NASHVILLE, 2019

My call was to face my vocation as a writer.

I couldn't do it. I was terrified.

Looking back, I think my years of running were at least in part a searching for that moment—I had no idea what it was—that would shake me and confront me with my own bullshit.

I didn't know it then but Joseph Campbell, from his studies of myths and legends, had a term for that moment too.

He called it the Meeting with the Mentor.

Day 97
MEETING WITH THE MENTOR

Luke had Obi-Wan Kenobi.

Rocky had Mick.

The original Achaean sage, Mentor (that was his name in Homer's *Iliad*), played this role for the Greeks besieging Troy.

The mentor's part in the hero's journey, according to Joseph Campbell, is to infuse the reluctant protagonist with the courage to leave the world he knows—the Ordinary World—and cross the threshold into the unknown, the Extraordinary World.

WRITING SEMINAR, NASHVILLE, 2019

Sometimes the mentor is inside ourselves.

A dream perhaps.

An intuition.

A moment of clarity.

A part of ourselves knows we can't remain where we are, stuck in a dead-end situation that will kill us by degrees if we don't get away.

But whether our heroes are counseled from without or within, the Refusal of the Call is overcome by the mentor's intervention and they, before they know it, are off to the races.

Day 98
THE CALL AND YOU

The concept of "the Call" is not confined to the written page or the characters you and I write. We as artists hear our own call, in our own lives.

An idea for a book pops into our head. An idea for a start-up. For a nonprofit.

The goddess is summoning us to an artistic/creative/entrepreneurial adventure.

WRITING SEMINAR, NASHVILLE, 2019

David Mamet comments eloquently on this phenomenon—the dual and simultaneous hero's journey of the protagonist on the page and the writer seeking to complete his or her work about that protagonist—in his book on drama and dramatic writing, *Three Uses of the Knife*.

"The agonies and transformation that our hero will and must undergo (and that we as writers strew before her) are mirrored and replicated by the passage you and I, the authors of our heroes' sufferings, will put ourselves through struggling to make our protagonist's story work."

WEEK FIFTEEN

CROSSING THE THRESHOLD

"The entire Spartan army, all twelve *lochoi* [regiments], had been drawn up on the plain to witness the march-out [of the Three Hundred to Thermopylae]. Each warrior of the expeditionary force stood garlanded, with his shield and spear at the carry, while his squire attended at his side bearing his armor and provisions. It was the month of Karneius and each man was due to receive his new cloak for the year. [King] Leonidas had ordered the issue discontinued for the Three Hundred. It would be an improvident use of the city's resources, he declared, to provide new garments for men who would have use of them for so brief a time."

GATES OF FIRE, P. 201–202

Act Two begins, in hero's journey terms, with a "crossing of the threshold." The hero leaves the Ordinary World behind and enters the Extraordinary World.

Alice steps through the looking glass. Dorothy is swept away from Kansas. Captain Miller and his squad set out on their search for Private Ryan.

From this point on, there will be no turning back. And nothing will be the same for any of them.

Day 100
CROSSING THE THRESHOLD
CHANGES EVERYTHING

Sometimes our hero is dragged kicking and screaming across the threshold, as Odysseus was when he was drafted for the Trojan War.

Sometimes our protagonist leaps in with both feet, as you or I might when we fall in love. Sometimes our hero willingly leaves behind a hated world or a despised self, like the character of student radical Pasha Antipov in *Doctor Zhivago*.

WRITING SEMINAR, NASHVILLE, 2019

There's a great moment in Chuck Palahniuk/David Fincher's *Fight Club*. Our narrator-without-a-name (Edward Norton) has fallen under the spell of his new friend and potential mentor Tyler Durden (Brad Pitt). And he needs a place to stay. (His own condo has just been blown up in a mysterious explosion.)

"Ask me," Tyler challenges him. "Say it."

"What do you mean?"

"Say you want to stay at my place."

It takes our hero ten tries before he can finally spit this out. He's scared. He knows crossing the threshold will change everything.

Day 101
OUR HERO BECOMES A DIFFERENT PERSON ACROSS THE THRESHOLD

Michael Corleone (Al Pacino) crosses the threshold when he guns down gangster Virgil Sollozzo and crooked police captain McCluskey in *The Godfather*. Before this moment, Michael had been a clean-cut, decorated WWII vet, engaged to his Mayflower-American fiancée Kay Adams and headed for a safe, all-American life.

Across the threshold, this new Michael is capable of actions he would never have dreamed of before.

UNPUBLISHED BLACK IRISH JAB, "CROSSING THE THRESHOLD"

Screenwriting guru Blake Snyder called this part of a story "fun and games." What he meant is that the narrative becomes suddenly energized and delivers to the audience or reader, for a time, the romance or horror or chills and thrills they came for.

Why has this become possible?

Because the hero has become a new person, charged with a voltage (of hope or terror or greed or revenge) that energizes every element of the story.

STEVEN PRESSFIELD

Day 102
OUR HERO IS SEEN AS DIFFERENT ACROSS THE THRESHOLD

The ultimate threshold-crosser in movies of the past forty years has to be Michael Dorsey/Dorothy Michaels (Dustin Hoffman) in *Tootsie*. Remember the scene when he/she enters the Russian Tea Room in New York, dressed and made up for the first time as a woman, and ensconces herself in a booth beside her agent George Fields (played by the film's director Sydney Pollack) who has no idea who this strange female is?

"It's me, George."

"What?"

"Your favorite client, Michael Dorsey."

"Oh God. I begged you to get some therapy."

UNPUBLISHED BLACK IRISH JAB, "CROSSING THE THRESHOLD"

The change in our hero across the threshold may be subtle. It may be perceived by others largely unconsciously. But on some level, they recognize our hero not as the person he or she was, but as some new, evolving, mutating version of him or herself.

OUR HERO SEES HIMSELF DIFFERENTLY ACROSS THE THRESHOLD

It isn't just other characters who react to our changed hero across the threshold. The hero himself or herself recognizes the change.

One of the reasons *Breaking Bad* made Bryan Cranston a star was that the story gave his character, Walter White/Heisenberg, so many juicy moments to show he had gone from mild-mannered milquetoast to All-Time Scary Bad Guy.

The shaved skull.

The porkpie hat.

The shades.

"I'm not in the meth business. I'm in the empire business."

UNPUBLISHED BLACK IRISH JAB, "CROSSING THE THRESHOLD"

Actors love those moments. They live for those moments.

Readers of novels do too.

When you and I write our characters across the threshold, it's our job to give 'em to them.

Day 104
"LAWRENCE, DO YOU KNOW YOU'RE A TRAITOR?"

Our hero, Lieutenant T.E. Lawrence (Peter O'Toole), has trekked into the desert to find Prince Feisal (Alec Guinness), leader of the Arab revolt. Lawrence sits, this evening, in the royal tent, beside his British Army superior, Colonel Harry Brighton (Anthony Quayle). Brighton is urging Feisal to put his Bedouin fighters under British command.

> LAWRENCE
> (to Brighton)
> I'm sorry, sir, but you're wrong.
> (to Feisal)
> My lord, your book [the *Koran*] is right.
> "The desert is an ocean in which no oar is
> dipped." And on that ocean the Bedouin
> go where they please and strike where they
> please. This is the way the Bedouin has
> always fought. And this is the way you must
> fight now!

> BRIGHTON
> Lawrence, do you know you're a traitor?

WRITING SEMINAR, NASHVILLE, 2019

Our heroes must all become "traitors" once they have crossed their thresholds—traitors to their prior selves, but patriots to the new selves they will become.

Day 105
THE THRESHOLD MOMENT IN NONFICTION

We cited earlier Elizabeth Gilbert's famous TED talk. That's not fiction. It's Ms. Gilbert's true story. But that talk had a threshold moment, just like a novel.

"The result of which is that everywhere I go now, people treat me like I'm doomed. Seriously—doomed, doomed!"

The moment came with the success of *Eat, Pray, Love*. Ms. Gilbert had crossed the threshold into the Land of Success and Fame.

UNPUBLISHED BLACK IRISH JAB, "CROSSING THE THRESHOLD"

And just like a character in a novel or a movie ...

1. Everyone else suddenly saw Ms. Gilbert differently.

2. Ms. Gilbert herself recognized that something had changed and that she was no longer the person she had been.

3. There was no going back.

WEEK SIXTEEN

FEAR

Day 106
RESISTANCE = FEAR

Resistance is experienced as fear; the degree of fear equates to the strength of Resistance. The more fear we feel about a specific enterprise, the more certain we can be that that enterprise is important to us and to the growth of our soul.

That's why we feel so much Resistance. If it meant nothing to us, there'd be no Resistance.

THE WAR OF ART, P. 40

The words we hear in our head when we experience Resistance take many forms. They may tell us we're a bum; we have no right to dream the dreams we dream. They may seek to convince us that everything good has already been done. Who are we, the voice may ask, to imagine we can do something original or daring or great?

The idiom Resistance uses on us may vary, but the emotion it presents is always the same—fear.

The degree to which we can overcome our fear is the degree to which we will overcome Resistance.

Day 107
FEAR IS GOOD

Are you paralyzed with fear? That's a good sign.

Fear is good. Like self-doubt, fear is an indicator. Fear tells us what we have to do.

Remember our rule of thumb: The more scared we are of a work or calling, the more certain we can be that we have to do it.

THE WAR OF ART, P. 51

When I consider a new project, the first question I ask myself is, "How scared am I of doing this?"

The answer I want to get is, "Scared shitless."

The fear with which a potential new book or start-up or enterprise strikes us is directly proportional to how important that enterprise is to the evolution of our soul.

Big fear = big dream.

The more scared we are, the better.

Day 108
FEAR DOESN'T GO AWAY

Henry Fonda was still throwing up before each stage performance, even when he was seventy-five. In other words, fear doesn't go away. The warrior and the artist live by the same code of necessity, which dictates that the battle must be fought anew every day.

THE WAR OF ART, P. 14

I get asked sometimes, "Does Resistance ever get easier?"

Answer: no.

What does help is the knowledge that we have beaten it in the past, so we know we can beat it again in the present.

But no, it never goes away.

And no, it never gets any easier.

Day 109
SELF-DOUBT IS GOOD

The voice in our head tells us we can't do it. Even if we've succeeded a hundred times in the past, the voice tells us this time we'll fall on our face.

Maddening, ain't it?

Why doesn't past success translate into present self-confidence? Why do even the most competent among us feel crippled with self-doubt?

WRITING SEMINAR, NASHVILLE, 2019

Remember, when we hear the voice of self-doubt in our head, that that voice is not us.

That voice is Resistance.

Its strength is equal and opposite to the power of our dream—of the work we wish to bring forth, the change we wish to effect in our lives.

The more self-doubt we feel, the more powerful the dream inside us…and the more certain we can be that we have to live it out.

Day 110
PANIC IS GOOD

Our greatest fear is fear of success. When we are succeeding—that is, when we have begun to overcome our self-doubt and self-sabotage, when we are advancing in our craft and evolving to a higher level... that's when panic strikes.

When we experience panic in the middle of a project—even if there's a real reason for panic, like we've just totally blown up our Act Two—it doesn't mean that we're worthless or hopeless or have no business attempting the work that we have set forth upon.

It means we're about to cross a threshold.

It means we're poised on the doorstep of a higher plane.

DO THE WORK, P. 76–77 [HARDBACK]

We advance as artists in a stairstep pattern. It's not a smooth upward slope. It's jigs and jags. It's plateaus and leaps.

Panic strikes when we're about to make a leap.

Day 111
THE USES OF FEAR

Like a magnetized needle floating on a surface of oil, Resistance will unfailingly point to true North—meaning that calling or action it most wants to stop us from doing.

We can use this. We can use it as a compass. We can navigate by Resistance, letting it guide us to that calling or action that we must follow before all others.

THE WAR OF ART, P. 12

Have you ever watched *Inside the Actors Studio*? When guests are asked, "What factors make you take a specific role?" they almost always answer with some version of, "I take a part because it scares me. Because I know it's going to make me stretch."

Resistance is felt as fear. The more fear we feel, the bigger the Resistance. And the bigger the Resistance, the bigger the dream.

Take the dream.

Day 112
RESISTANCE IS FUELED BY FEAR

Resistance has no strength of its own. Every ounce of juice it possesses comes from us. We feed it with power by our fear of it.

Master that fear and we conquer Resistance.

THE WAR OF ART, P. 16

A bully will back down when confronted by any opponent willing to stand her ground.

Resistance is a bully.

We defeat it not by wrestling it or punching it or kicking it (those only make it stronger), but by turning toward our own fear and dismissing it.

STEVEN PRESSFIELD

WEEK SEVENTEEN

THE HERO'S JOURNEY, PART ONE

Day 113
STAR WARS

The first *Star Wars* came out about ten years before I started working in Tinseltown. By that time, the concept of "the hero's journey" (upon which George Lucas had patterned Luke Skywalker's odyssey) had permeated Hollywood top to bottom.

NOBODY WANTS TO READ YOUR SH*T, P. 65

A book I highly recommend for any writer in fiction or film is Christopher Vogler's *The Writer's Journey*. Vogler was a story exec at Disney, Fox 2000, and Warner Bros. during the era when the concept of the hero's journey dominated everything in Movieland, and he writes with brilliance and concision about its impact—narratively, politically, and commercially.

You will never look at Dorothy and *The Wizard of Oz* (or any other story) the same way after reading Vogler's *The Writer's Journey*.

Day 114
WHAT IS A HERO ANYWAY?

The word "hero" can be off-putting. It sounds like something musclebound and macho...and very definitely male. Let's disabuse ourselves of that notion when we speak here of the hero's journey.

The "hero" is you and I, male or female.

The hero is the central character of the story.

You are the hero of your life, as I am the hero of mine.

Our journey in spirit is our hero's journey.

INSTAGRAM SERIES, "THE WARRIOR ARCHETYPE", 2021

The three defining characteristics of the protagonist in any story apply to you and me in our real-life hero's journeys.

1. The hero embodies the story's theme.

2. In the climax, the hero (and nobody else) takes the resolving action.

3. The story ends, or moves on to its next evolution, when the hero's issues are resolved and no sooner.

THE HERO'S JOURNEY ITSELF

The hero's journey is the Ur-Story of every individual from Adam and Eve to Ziggy Stardust.

NOBODY WANTS TO READ YOUR SH*T, P. 65–66

Cue up any movie from *Casablanca* to *The Martian* to *Get Out.* Read any novel from *Huckleberry Finn* to *The Corrections* to *Never Let Me Go.* At the heart of each, in one form or another, you will find the hero's journey.

Day 116
THE HERO'S JOURNEY, DEEPER VERSION

Beyond its utility as a cheat sheet for writing hit novels or movies, what exactly is the "hero's journey"?

According to C.G. Jung, the hero's journey is a component of the collective unconscious. Joseph Campbell identified it in the myths and legends of virtually every culture on earth.

The hero's journey arose, both men speculated, from the accumulated experience of the human race. The hero's journey acts as a template or a user's manual. It tells us, "This is how life works. This is the road map to the way your own saga will unfold."

NOBODY WANTS TO READ YOUR SH*T, P. 68

In other words, the hero's journey is a scenario that plays out inevitably, over and over, not just in our fiction but in our own lives.

If you're reading this, you are almost certainly in the middle of your own hero's journey, whether you realize it or not, whether you like it or not.

Day 117
A READING LIST
FOR THE HERO'S JOURNEY

Required reading: Joseph Campbell's *The Hero with a Thousand Faces*, C.G. Jung's essay *The Structure of the Unconscious* and his book *Symbols of Transformation*, and, as we mentioned earlier, for the real Movieland nitty-gritty, Christopher Vogler's *The Writer's Journey*.

NOBODY WANTS TO READ YOUR SH*T, P. 68

Add Bill Moyers' six-part PBS series, *Joseph Campbell and the Power of Myth*. And, of course, *Star Wars, The Wizard of Oz* and *The Odyssey*.

STEVEN PRESSFIELD

Day 118
THE ARCHETYPAL HERO'S JOURNEY

There's a reason why an all-consuming physical/spiritual/evolutionary life-journey is called an "odyssey."

It's because Homer's *Odyssey*, the story of Odysseus's ten-year ordeal in the aftermath of the Trojan War, is the primal and ultimate "hero's journey."

UNPUBLISHED BLACK IRISH JAB, "THE HERO'S JOURNEY"

My three key takeaways from the *Odyssey*:

1. It's about a journey home. A return to the place from which the hero started.

2. The hero does return. He gets home. But he has been changed utterly by his ordeal.

3. Throughout Odysseus's journey, he is accompanied by the goddess Athena. She counsels him. She rescues him. She intervenes repeatedly on his behalf.

You and I have guardian goddesses at our shoulder as well.

Do you believe me?

Day 119
THE HERO'S JOURNEY
IN OUR OWN LIVES

I have a theory about the hero's journey. We all have one. We have many, in fact. But our primary hero's journey as artists is the passage we live out, in real life, before we find our calling.

The hero's journey is the search for that calling.

On our hero's journey, we see, we experience, we suffer. We learn.

On our hero's journey, we acquire a history that is ours alone. It's a secret history, a private history, a personal history. No one has it but us. No one knows it but us. This secret history is the most valuable possession we hold, or ever will hold. We will draw upon it for the rest of our lives.

THE ARTIST'S JOURNEY, P. 6

You can live out your hero's journey in a cubicle. You can live it out like Proust did, under the covers in your own bed.

But live it out, you shall.

WEEK EIGHTEEN

THE HERO'S JOURNEY, REAL-LIFE VERSION

Day 120
THE HERO'S JOURNEY
IS A LIVING, BREATHING THING

The hero's journey template in our psyches exerts a powerful, almost irresistible pressure on the individual to *live it out in real life*.

What makes us leave our hometown and head to the Big Apple? Why do we enlist in the Special Forces? What is happening beneath the surface when we meet a stranger on a plane and follow him to Argentina?

The hero's journey software in our heads is demanding to be lived out.

The blanks are insisting on being filled in.

THE ARTIST'S JOURNEY, P. 8

Why do we have stories? Why do we need stories?

Because stories are models of the interior/exterior journey(s) that all of us find ourselves upon, over and over, in our real lives. We read *Madame Bovary* or watch *Apocalypse Now* to help us understand the dramas in which we are the featured players and in which the stakes for us, just like the heroes we read about in novels and myths and legends, are life and death.

Day 121
THE HERO'S JOURNEY
IS A FILL-IN-THE-BLANKS PROPOSITION

The hero (_____) receives the Call when (_____) walks into his/her life and does/says (_____).

Hero crosses the Threshold at (_____) place and (_____) time. He/she encounters Monsters (_____) and is assisted by Allies (_____).

Hero returns safely at last to (_____), the place from which she/he started, by means of a (_____), bringing for the people the gift of (_____), hard-won from his/her experiences.

THE ARTIST'S JOURNEY, **P. 9**

The hero's journey is a template. It's a pattern. It has a beginning, a middle, and an end. It has a shape. It has a contour.

What it does *not* have, at least in its primal form within our psyches, are specifics. It does not have particulars.

You and I will fill those in (or life itself will do it for us) as we live out our journeys in real time and real life.

Day 122
MY HERO'S JOURNEY

My own hero's journey lasted about two and a half years—from age twenty-six to twenty-nine. It hit every beat in the myth, by the numbers and in sequence.

I had no idea at the time of course that what I was experiencing might be called a hero's journey. I had never heard of the hero's journey.

What was clear to me was that something was happening, and that something was a runaway train I couldn't stop or slow down or get off. What was clear too was when it ended. I knew the exact moment. I could feel it.

THE ARTIST'S JOURNEY, P. 10–11

My hero's journey came at a heavy cost. I knew it would take me years to recover, to re-find my footing in the world. I didn't care. The trip was worth it.

Why?

Because I now had a history that was mine alone. I had an ordeal that I had survived and a passage that I had paid for with my own blood. Nobody knew about this passage but me. Nobody would ever know, nor did I feel the slightest urge to communicate it. This was mine, and nobody could ever take it away from me.

I had punched my ticket. I had filled in the blanks.

Day 123
THE VILLAIN OF MY HERO'S JOURNEY

The devil during my period of exile was Resistance.

Resistance was the dragon I couldn't slay, the witch's curse that held me spellbound. I couldn't see it. I had no idea it even existed. Resistance massacred me from ambush and mowed me down from concealment.

UNPUBLISHED BLACK IRISH JAB, "EXILE"

In Jewish mysticism, Resistance is called the yetzer hara. This entity is the mortal foe of the neshama, the soul, and of the manifested spirit—you and I—who is seeking to connect to this higher entity.

I said in 2002 in *The War of Art* that Resistance will bury you, and nothing I've seen or experienced in the intervening years has prompted me to revise that statement.

Day 124
EXILE

Exile, say the Gnostics, is the human condition. I agree. In the Kabbalistic metaphor, the self is depicted as a vessel created by the Almighty to contain light—the light of consciousness, the light of the soul.

But the vessel is cracked.

The object of life on earth, say the mystics, is to repair those cracks and return the vessel to such a state as can, again, contain the divine light.

That's how I feel.

That's what my life feels like.

UNPUBLISHED BLACK IRISH JAB, "EXILE"

The hero's journey is a passage through exile. Act One is the ejection from a safe but ultimately sterile Eden. Act Two is the harrowing passage across the unknown. Act Three is the return home.

The point is: There is a return. There is a home.

So if your sense of your own life is one of exile, don't panic.

You are on the path.

THE HERO'S JOURNEY IS AN INITIATION

Make that a *self*-initiation.

The hero's journey ends when, like Odysseus, we return home to Ithaca, to the place from which we started. We wash up on shore. We have survived. We have come home.

Now what?

The passage that comes next is the Artist's Journey.

The Artist's Journey comes after the Hero's Journey.

Everything that has happened to us up to this point is rehearsal for us to act, now, as our true self and to find and speak in our true voice.

THE ARTIST'S JOURNEY, P. 6–7

The Artist's Journey is the process of self-discovery that follows the hero's journey.

It will last as long as we're alive, and maybe longer.

Day 126
THE HERO'S JOURNEY
AS A FORM OF SELF-TORMENT

What was/is your Act Two, your medium of passage?

Are you an alcoholic, a substance abuser, a sex addict? Is your drug of choice abuse of yourself or others, or do you prefer the role of victim? Are you addicted to drama, to heartbreak, to illness? Are you violent, depressed, TFU?

Or are you a normal, garden-variety Jane or Joe, who hasn't hurt anybody or committed any Class-A felonies—but who just can't embrace your Real Dream, or sometimes even remember where you put it.

It's okay.

The state of frustration and dissatisfaction in which you find yourself is not hell. It's your hero's journey.

UNPUBLISHED BLACK IRISH JAB, EXILE

The hero's journey feels like hell to the hero. It's supposed to. That's why they call it the hero's journey.

WEEK NINETEEN

THE EXTRAORDINARY WORLD

When I was twenty-four, I quit a real-world job for the first time and set out to write a novel.

Four years later I was broke, divorced, etc., having in the interim crossed the United States thirteen times in my '65 Chevy van, supporting myself as, variously, a cab driver, bartender, tractor-trailer driver, oilfield roustabout, and migratory fruit picker. The last straw came on a gale-scoured highway near Amarillo, Texas, when a friend I had just made, a ranch hand who was traveling with his new wife and all their worldly goods in two paper bags, invited me to come with him to work cattle on his brother's spread east of Lubbock. For a few seconds I thought about it.

A cowboy.

Would that round out my American odyssey?

NOBODY WANTS TO READ YOUR SH*T, P. 41

When did you and I cross the threshold? When did we enter the Extraordinary World?

And have we, yet, gotten back?

A HOUSE IN THE CITY

In my late twenties, I lived for a winter in a boarding house in Durham, North Carolina, that was a halfway station for patients emerging from state mental hospitals. I wasn't a mental patient myself, but the law of metaphor had brought me to this place as surely as if I had been.

I began to wonder how I came to be in this house with these people. Why did I feel so at home? Was this my destiny?

Then one night I had a dream. In the dream I came into my room and found that my shirts had folded themselves neatly in my drawer (instead of being mashed together in their usual jumbled mess). My boots had crawled out from under the bed and had set themselves upright and tidy. They had shined themselves.

When I woke up, I thought, "I'm ambitious! I have ambition!"

TURNING PRO, P. 7–8

This was Call 9.0 for me. It came not from events but from a dream. I don't know about you, but in my life, dreams have been my greatest mentor.

Day 129
A HOUSE IN THE COUNTRY

I decided that I had to leave the halfway house. I found a cinderblock cabin along a highway in the country that rented for fifteen dollars a week. I still have a photo of that house. The house had no electricity, no toilet, no running water and no heat. I cooked my meals outdoors in back, over a fire of pine kindling that I collected from the woods.

I had started driving for the trucking company then, so it didn't matter too much where I lived. I was sleeping most nights in the truck's sleeper berth and eating my meals in cafes and truck stops on the road.

The reason I keep a photo of that house is that it changed my life. To find that house and to move into it was the first act I had taken as an adult that embraced the idea of ambition.

TURNING PRO, P. 8–9

In the Extraordinary World, we become a different person. We live in places that we never thought we'd live. We access parts of ourselves that we never knew existed.

It's terrifying living in the Extraordinary World, but it's self-empowering too. We are confronting our own Inner Villain. We are in our own Act Two.

STEVEN PRESSFIELD

Day 130
MY FIRST HERO

There was a redheaded cat who used to come around sometimes when I lived in that house in the country. He was a battle-scarred old tom who lived in the woods. On nights when I was home, I would cook supper over a little fire out back. The cat would materialize and sit across from me while I ate. I tried to toss him scraps of food but he wouldn't take them. He was nobody's pet.

There was no doubt in either of our minds which one of us was the superior being. There was no doubt which one could take care of himself and which one had his shit together.

I admired that redheaded cat. I wanted to be like him. I regarded his apparition as a good omen and a sign that, maybe, I was on the right path.

TURNING PRO, P. 10–11

Our villain is inside us during our own Act Two. Mine was my own Resistance.

The part of me that was fighting that villain was the part, I believe, that summoned that redheaded cat and brought him to me as a mentor and a role model.

MY SMITH-CORONA

What was really happening in that house in the country was I was hiding.

In the back of my Chevy van, under piles of junk and spare parts, sat my ancient Smith-Corona typewriter. Why didn't I throw it away? I certainly wasn't using it.

Fear and shame hung over me in that house, just as they permeated every cranny of the halfway house back in town. I was terrified of sitting down at that Smith-Corona and trying to write something and ashamed of myself because I knew that but was still too scared to act.

Everything I was doing in my outer life was a consequence and an expression of that terror and that shame.

TURNING PRO, P. 12

Resistance was my villain, but I couldn't see it or touch it. I had no idea it even existed.

In Act Two, the villain assaults the protagonist.

Day 132
MY DREAM EAGLE

I was sitting cross-legged when an eagle came and landed on my shoulders. The eagle merged with me and took off flying, so that my head became its head and my arms its wings. It felt completely authentic. I could feel the air under my wings, as solid as water feels when you row in it with an oar.

So this was how birds flew! I realized it was impossible for a bird to fall out of the sky; all it would have to do was extend its wings; the solid air would hold it up. "Hey!" I asked the eagle. "What am I supposed to be learning from this?"

A voice answered (silently): "You're supposed to learn that things that you think are nothing, as weightless as air, are actually powerful substantial forces, as real and as solid as earth. "

THE WAR OF ART, P. 130

On our hero's journey we seek mentors and allies. The most powerful ally I've ever found resides inside my own Self.

Read Robert Johnson's *Inner Work*. Pay attention to your dreams.

Around this time in my house in the country, I had this dream:

I was part of the crew of an aircraft carrier. Only the ship was stuck on dry land. The sailors felt this as a keen and constant distress. The only positive force was a Marine gunnery sergeant on board nicknamed "Largo."

Largo was one of those hard-core senior noncoms like the Burt Lancaster character in *From Here to Eternity*—the one guy on the ship who understands the problem, the tough old sarge who actually runs the show.

But where was Largo? I was standing miserably by the rail when the captain came over and started talking to me. It was his ship, but he didn't know how to get it off dry land. I was nervous, finding myself in conversation with the brass. The skipper didn't seem to notice. He just turned to me casually and said, "What the hell are we going to do, Largo?"

THE WAR OF ART, P. 128–129

Meetings with the Mentor have come almost always, for me, in my dreams.

WEEK TWENTY

CONFRONTING THE VILLAIN

Day 134
THE FIGHT BEGINS IN ACT TWO

"Our practice is to pickle at 2,500 feet above ground level, meaning drop the bombs and begin to pull out of the dive.

"Down we go. The altimeter passes 3,500, which is still pretty high, but the [enemy] runway is getting wider and wider in my windscreen and I'm getting the terrible feeling that something is wrong. Suddenly I realize my pickle figure is based on sea level, the reading for the airfields in Egypt [that we attacked this morning]. But we are [now, in the afternoon] at [airfield] T-4 on the Syrian plateau. Its altitude may be as high as 2,500 feet. All this goes through my mind in a fraction of a second.

"I drop my ordnance at 800 feet—way, way too low. I pull out at impossibly high G's and am saved only by the fact that my bombs are on delayed fuses, so they don't explode as my plane passes directly over the impact points."

ISRAELI FIGHTER PILOT "HEMI" SCHMUL FROM *THE LION'S GATE*, P. 166–167

In Act Two, our protagonist—meaning our self in real life as well—will find the ground shifting beneath him. Why?

Because our hero is now actively engaging the Villain, something he had avoided throughout his term in the Ordinary World, i.e., Act One.

Day 135
THE SECOND ACT
BELONGS TO THE VILLAIN

I learned this from my friend Randall Wallace (*Braveheart*), who learned it from Stephen Cannell, the maestro of a thousand plotlines from *The Rockford Files* to *Baretta* to *21 Jump Street*.

What Steve Cannell meant was bring the villain's effects on the hero into the foreground and keep them there. Why? Because the havoc and jeopardy they incite energize the story and keep it powering forward.

NOBODY WANTS TO READ YOUR SH*T, P. 76

The Second Act, or what David Mamet calls the "middle passage," is the marrow of the narrative, where all the juicy stuff of the hero's ordeal takes place.

What does this ordeal consist of? It consists of clashes with the villain as the villain seeks to obstruct the hero's pursuit of her or his intention.

Day 136
EVERY VILLAIN
IS A METAPHOR FOR RESISTANCE

Resistance is the universal and ultimate villain. Consider how this monster was described in *The War of Art*.

1. Resistance is insidious. It has no conscience. [It] is always lying and always full of shit.

2. Resistance is implacable. It cannot be reasoned with. Reduce it to a single cell and that cell will continue to attack.

3. Resistance is impersonal. It doesn't know who you are and it doesn't care. Resistance is a force of nature.

4. Resistance's goal is not to wound or disable. It aims to kill. When we fight Resistance, we are in a war to the death.

BLACK IRISH JAB #8, "BAD GUYS, PART TWO"

Write a villain that is as evil as Resistance (and shares its specific qualities) and you will be more than halfway to penning something great.

Day 137
THE SECOND ACT
BELONGS TO THE VILLAIN, PART TWO

The villain in *The Godfather* (at least the personified individual) is Virgil Sollozzo (Al Lettieri). Remember him? Here's what he does as the second act unfolds:

1. Sollozzo and the Tattaglia family kill Luca Brasi by garroting him in a hotel bar.

2. Sollozzo's gunmen attempt to assassinate Don Corleone.

3. When Don Corleone miraculously survives, Sollozzo's goons and his allies in the NYPD try to kill him in the hospital.

4. Sollozzo's menace forces the Corleone family to "go to the mattresses."

5. Sollozzo sends a package to the Corleones—a dead fish wrapped in Luca Brasi's bulletproof vest. "Luca Brasi sleeps with the fishes."

BLACK IRISH JAB #7, "BAD GUYS, PART ONE"

Even after Sollozzo is killed by Michael in the Italian restaurant, the villain continues to dominate (and energize) the second act, culminating in the Tommy-gun murder of Sonny Corleone (James Caan) on the causeway.

The second act should be packed with the villain's threats, machinations, and attacks. The hero should have to react and react and react again.

Day 138
"GIMME MORE BUMPS"

I wrote a screenplay once for a producer who called the incursions of the villain "bumps."

"We need more bumps," he would tell me. "Gimme a bump here on page 41 and another on page 48. Never let ten pages go by without a bump."

He was right.

When you and I find ourselves struggling in the belly of our story, we could do worse than to take a cue from this producer or from Steve Cannell.

Give us some bumps.

The Second Act belongs to the villain.

"WRITING WEDNESDAYS," STEVENPRESSFIELD.COM, 1/3/18

It is not enough, however, to simply pile on the bumps.

The bumps must escalate. Each bump must raise the stakes for the hero. Each must evolve out of the bump that came before and be a consequence and an elaboration of that bump.

Each bump must take the hero deeper into the marrow of the story.

ESCALATING BUMPS IN *CHINATOWN*

Private investigator Jake Gittes (Jack Nicholson) is the hero of Robert Towne and Roman Polanski's *Chinatown*. Consider the bumps he encounters starting in Act One.

Jake is hired by Mrs. Evelyn Mulwray (Diane Ladd) to tail her husband, whom she suspects is having an affair. Suddenly a second Mrs. Mulwray appears. She is the real Mrs. Mulwray (Faye Dunaway). She declares the first woman a fraud and threatens to sue Jake.

Mulwray is murdered. Investigating, Jake is shot at, nearly drowned, and beaten up. His nose is nearly cut off by two Bad Guys who apparently work for a Bigger Bad Guy.

Jake is beaten up in the orchard.

He's shot at and nearly killed at the rest home.

I've left a bunch of bumps out, but you get the idea.

UNPUBLISHED BLACK IRISH JAB, "SECOND ACT HORRORS"

Each bump leads directly and inevitably to the next bump. Each one peels back a deeper layer of the onion—meaning the villain's villainy, both in the past and in the present.

THE PLOT THICKENS

The bumps must not escalate simply quantitatively, in terms of violence or even in terms of stakes. They should also ascend qualitatively (or rather descend, as in "toward evil") in terms of *depth of meaning*.

UNPUBLISHED BLACK IRISH JAB, "SECOND ACT HORRORS"

Remember, we're talking here about our own navigation of the tricky terrain of our second act. We must ask ourselves of our own story:

Is our hero confronting the villain throughout Act Two?

Does each bump escalate? Does each force the hero to dig deeper into his own resources? Does each bump pull the hero further into the mystery, into the human connection with the tale?

Does each bump escalate to a deeper level of meaning?

WEEK TWENTY-ONE

ASPECTS OF THE VILLAIN

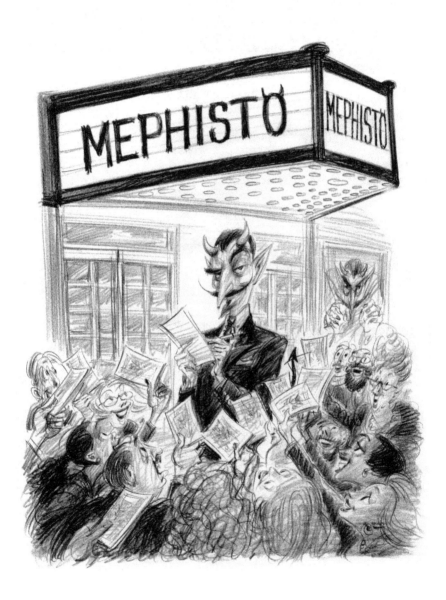

Day 141
WHAT EXACTLY IS A VILLAIN?

Why do we need an antagonist at all? Why not have everyone in our story be a hero?

Because without a villain there is no story.

The definition of "story" is a clash between opposites that produces greater insight on the part of the reader into the nature of life.

UNPUBLISHED BLACK IRISH JAB, "BAD GUYS, PART FIVE"

Every story must be *about something*. It must have a theme.

Casablanca: Better to sacrifice oneself (or one's personal happiness) for the greater good than to live a life of narrow self-interest.

Rocky: Anyone can be a champion, at least on their own terms, if he or she is only given an honest shot.

The hero embodies the theme.

The villain embodies the counter-theme.

Without gravity, we could not walk. Without a villain, we can't have a story.

EVERYBODY LOVES THE VILLAIN

Shakespeare, Milton, and Dante all understood villains. They loved villains. Their villains are their greatest creations.

The Bible is loaded with spectacular villains, as are all cultural myths from the *Mahabharata* to the Epic of Gilgamesh to the saga of Siegfried.

Great villains eclipse even the heroes who vanquish them.

Flash Gordon was a pale shadow alongside Ming the Merciless.

Clarice Starling was cool, but who could forget Hannibal Lecter?

The villain not only steals *Paradise Lost* but walks off with the most unforgettable line.

> SATAN
> Better to reign in hell than serve in heaven.

BLACK IRISH JAB #7, "BAD GUYS, PART ONE"

When in doubt in Act Two, come back to the villain. He will save you.

Day 143
THE VILLAIN
EMBODIES THE COUNTER-THEME

If our hero's aim is to save the world, our villain's object is to destroy it.

Whatever the protagonist wants, the antagonist wants the opposite.

BLACK IRISH JAB #8, "BAD GUYS, PART TWO"

When you and I find ourselves struggling in Act Two, it's often because we haven't truly defined our story's theme for ourselves and have failed to:

1. Make the hero embody the theme, and

2. Make the villain embody the counter-theme.

If we can lick this problem, everything else will fall into place.

THE VILLAIN IS NOT ALWAYS A PERSON

Or even a creature.

The villain can be an obsession, a fear, a desire, a dream, a conception of reality. It can be an idea.

The villain in *Blade Runner 1978* would seem at first glance to be the replicants, who have escaped off-world and come to Earth sowing destruction. But the real villain is an idea—the unholy notion of creating faux-human slave labor.

This is the same villain, by the way, as in *Birth of a Nation* (2016), *12 Years a Slave*, and *The Help*.

BLACK IRISH JAB #7, "BAD GUYS, PART ONE"

There are (at least) three types of villain.

External, like the Alien or the shark in *Jaws*.

Societal, like racism or homophobia.

And interior—a fear, a belief, an obsession that exists entirely within the protagonist's head.

Day 145
ELEMENTS OF A GREAT VILLAIN

What qualities do the shark in *Jaws*, the Alien, the Terminator and all other great villains have in common?

1. They cannot be reasoned with.

2. They cannot be appealed to on the basis of justice, fair play, or the idea of right and wrong.

3. They are driven internally, relentlessly to achieve their ends.

> KYLE REESE (MICHAEL BIEHN)
> Listen, and understand! That Terminator is
> out there! It can't be bargained with. It can't
> be reasoned with. It doesn't feel pity, or
> remorse, or fear. And it absolutely will not
> stop...ever, until you are dead!

BLACK IRISH JAB #7, "BAD GUYS, PART ONE"

Whether our villain is external, societal, or internal, it must be relentless, implacable, and un-appealable-to, like the antagonists above.

THE VILLAIN DOESN'T THINK
HE'S THE VILLAIN

When you read these lines from Aaron Sorkin's *A Few Good Men*, see them, if you can, as honorable and noble and coming from a posture of pure, selfless patriotism.

> COL. JESSUP (JACK NICHOLSON)
> Son, we live in a world that has walls, and
> those walls have to be guarded by men with
> guns. Who's gonna do it? You?…I have nei-
> ther the time nor the inclination to explain
> myself to a man who rises and sleeps under
> the blanket of the very freedom that I pro-
> vide, and then questions the manner in
> which I provide it. Otherwise, I suggest you
> pick up a weapon, and stand a post. Either
> way, I don't give a damn what you think
> you are entitled to.

BLACK IRISH JAB #7, "BAD GUYS, PART ONE"

In the villain's eyes, he's the hero.

To him, the hero is the villain.

The Bad Guy is just following his own moral vision of reality. He's just trying to do his job.

GIVE YOUR VILLAIN
A GREAT VILLAIN SPEECH

> GORDON GEKKO (MICHAEL DOUGLAS)
> The point is…that greed, for lack of a better
> word, is good. Greed is right, greed works.
> Greed clarifies, cuts through, and captures
> the essence of the evolutionary spirit…And
> greed, you mark my words, will not only
> save Teldar Paper, but that other malfunc-
> tioning corporation called the USA.

A great villain speech displays no repentance. The devil makes his case with full slash and swagger. His cause is just and he knows it.

A great villain speech possesses eloquence. The Bad Guy expresses himself with wit and style.

Lastly, a great villain speech is marked by impeccable logic. Like the one above from Oliver Stone's *Wall Street,* it is, at least upon first hearing, convincing and compelling.

NOBODY WANTS TO READ YOUR SH*T, **P. 108**

When we hear a great villain speech, we should think despite ourselves, "I gotta say, the dude makes sense."

WEEK TWENTY-TWO

THE AGGRESSIVE ATTITUDE

Day 148
THE AGGRESSIVE ATTITUDE

"Always attack. Even in defense, attack. The attacking arm possesses the initiative and thus commands the action. To attack makes men brave; to defend makes them timorous."

ALEXANDER IN *THE VIRTUES OF WAR*, P. 177 [HARDBACK]

Pushback is inherent in the life of the artist and the entrepreneur. We call it Resistance for a reason.

Because it resists.

It resists our wishes.

It resists our needs.

It resists our intentions.

In confronting this resisting force, there is no substitute for aggression, for a vision of the wider picture, and for perseverance.

STEVEN PRESSFIELD

Day 149
DVEKUT BA MESIMA

The following quote is from Lieutenant Giora Romm, the first fighter-pilot ace [shooting down five enemy planes] of the Israel Air Force:

"The best of the best were not motivated by money or fame. Their aim was to serve the nation, to sacrifice their lives if necessary. At the military boarding school I attended, it was assumed that every graduate would volunteer for a fighting unit, the more elite the better. But what was even more powerful were the precepts the school hammered into our skulls.

"First: complete the mission.

"The phrase in Hebrew is *Dvekut baMesima.*

"Mesima is 'mission,' dvekut means 'glued to.' The mission is everything. At all costs, it must be carried through to completion."

THE LION'S GATE, P. 14–15

Readers sometimes take me to task for making so many analogies to battles and actions of war. But you and I are warriors. We are on a mission, no less than fighter pilots and tank commanders, and the stakes for us, as for them, are life and death.

Day 150
INTANGIBLES

"Never forget, gentlemen, that you command Athenians and that those elements which make our countrymen great are intangible—daring and intelligence, adaptability and esprit. Put these in the bank for me and I will get you all the ships you need."

TIDES OF WAR, P. 260 [HARDBACK]

It's okay to sing softly or to strike a note of languor or melancholy. But behind it, the stance must always be aggressive.

STEVEN PRESSFIELD

Day 151
THINKING BIG

When we're starting out in any field, timidity can get the best of us.

"I can't write a novel. Let me try a short story."

"Let me try a blog...or an Instagram post."

"Lemme try a tweet."

UNPUBLISHED BLACK IRISH JAB, "THINK IN CAMPAIGNS"

When I started out as a junior copywriter at Benton & Bowles in New York, I used to bring in the teensiest, tiniest, most timorous ideas to my boss, Ed Hannibal. His head would explode with frustration.

"What is this you're bringing me, Steve? This idea is the size of a postage stamp! Get outa here and come back with something *big*!"

Ed's primary mantra:

"Don't think in ads. Think in campaigns."

BRAVE AS A LION

"He is sitting across from me, this young guy, redheaded, brave as a lion, the kind of flier every squadron commander dreams about.

"'Goddammit!,' I tell him. 'Do you think I can let you fly [as recklessly as] that? You almost killed yourself and [your wingman]!'

"From [this young man] I am learning an important lesson. I had believed a squadron commander could know his men as fliers only. Now Schmul tells me of his father, whom he never saw, never knew, murdered by Arabs ten days before he was born. He grew up with this.

"You have to know what drives your people."

MAJOR RAN RONEN FROM *THE LION'S GATE*, P. 170 [PAPERBACK]

Ran Ronen was one of the greatest flying commanders in the history of the Israel Air Force. He forgave young lieutenant Schmul's wildness in combat because he valued aggressiveness so highly.

"I would rather have to rein in the fiery warhorse," Moshe Dayan once said, "than prod the reluctant mule."

Day 153
AGONY

"Those who do not understand war believe it contention between armies, friend against foe. No. Rather friend and foe duel as one against an unseen antagonist, whose name is Fear, and seek, even entwined in death, to mount to that promontory whose ensign is honor."

ALEXANDER IN *THE VIRTUES OF WAR,* P. 5–6 [HARDBACK]

Our English word agony comes from the Greek *agon*, which means contention, as in the struggle of man against man on the wrestling mat or the field of combat.

Agonist is one who participates in this agon, as *protagonist* is seen as hero and *antagonist* is opponent.

The Greeks believed that agon was sacred—a crucible that refined ore into gold. The price of that gold is pain and ultimately, in the best sense, self-abnegation, self-effacement.

Agony.

Aggressive agony.

Good agony.

Day 154
EN BRERA

"Now I'm going to tell you something very severe. *En brera.* 'No alternative.' The battle tomorrow will be life and death. Each man will assault to the end, taking no account of casualties. There will be no retreat. No halt, no hesitation. Only forward assault."

GENERAL ISRAEL TAL FROM *THE LION'S GATE*, P. 181 [PAPERBACK]

I cited this quote earlier, in the context of the stop-for-nothing attitude that is so critical in the writing of a first draft. But it applies across the board for any artist or entrepreneur embarking on a project that means the world to her.

The enemy between our ears is implacable. We must tell ourselves, with General Tal, "No halt, no hesitation. Only forward assault."

WEEK TWENTY-THREE

THE OPINION OF OTHERS

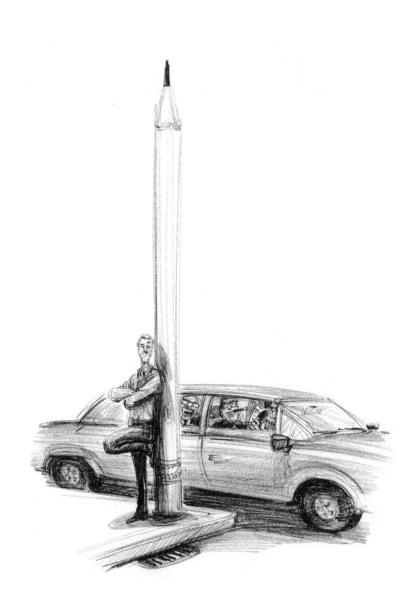

Day 155
THE OPINIONS OF OTHERS

The artist cannot look to others to validate his efforts or his calling. If you don't believe me, ask Van Gogh, who produced masterpiece after masterpiece and never found a buyer in his whole life.

THE WAR OF ART, P. 150–151

My business partner Shawn Coyne has a term for this. He calls it 3PV—third-party validation.

This is not, in his lexicon, a positive term.

Day 156
"I SENT MYSELF TO BED
WITHOUT SUPPER"

"From that day, I vowed never to squander a moment's care over the good opinion of others. May they rot in hell. You have heard of my abstemiousness in matters of food and sex. Here is why: I punished myself. If I caught my thoughts straying to another's opinion of me, I sent myself to bed without supper. As for women, I likewise permitted myself none. I missed no few meals, and no small pleasure, before I brought this vice under control."

ALEXANDER IN *THE VIRTUES OF WAR*, P. 175 [HARDBACK]

Looking to the good opinion of others is natural. It's in our DNA. Surely it has served (and still serves) in the evolutionary sense to make us good tribespeople, reliable teammates, dependable confederates.

That does not make it any less of a vice.

THERE IS NO TRIBE

The amateur dreads becoming who she really is because she fears that this new person will be judged by others as "different." The tribe will declare us "weird" or "queer" or "crazy."

The tribe will reject us.

Here's the truth: the tribe doesn't give a shit. There is no tribe. That gang or posse that we imagine is sustaining us is in fact a conglomeration of individuals who are just as fucked up as we are and just as terrified. Each individual is so caught up in his own bullshit that he doesn't have two seconds to worry about yours or mine, or to reject or diminish us because of it.

When we truly understand that the tribe doesn't give a damn, we're free. There is no tribe, and there never was. Our lives are entirely up to us.

TURNING PRO, P. 68

The only tribe whose opinion matters is the one looking back at us in the mirror.

Day 158
PROSTITUTION

To labor in the arts for any reason other than love is prostitution.

THE WAR OF ART, P. 151

Don't get me wrong. I've sold out. I've labored for Mister Charley. I've taken work I wouldn't tell my mother about and brought the check on a beeline to the bank.

But I was a whore to do it, and I can't say a word in my defense.

Day 159
TAKING IT PERSONALLY

The professional cannot take rejection personally because to do so reinforces Resistance.

Editors are not the enemy. Critics are not the enemy. Resistance is the enemy. The battle is inside our own heads. We cannot let external criticism, even if it's true, fortify our internal foe. That foe is strong enough already.

THE WAR OF ART, P. 87–88

Evaluating our work by the opinions of others is a form of Resistance. Hemingway famously said that if we believe the critics when they tell us we're good, we have to believe them when they tell us we're bad.

Day 160
THE AMATEUR LIVES
BY THE OPINIONS OF OTHERS

The amateur allows his worth and identity to be defined by others. The amateur craves third-party validation.

The amateur is tyrannized by his imagined conception of what is expected of him. He is imprisoned by what he believes he ought to think, how he ought to look, what he ought to do, and who he ought to be.

TURNING PRO, P. 56

When we turn pro, we accept responsibility for who we are. We step out of the shadow of ought-to-be and should-be and how-we-are-expected-to-be.

Day 161
MY FAVORITE SAMURAI

"I fight for the fight alone, serve for the serving alone, tramp for the tramping alone."

TELAMON OF ARCADIA IN *A MAN AT ARMS*, EARLY DRAFT, P. 297

My favorite character in Akira Kurosawa's *Seven Samurai* is "Kyuzo" played by Seiji Miyaguchi. Do you remember him? He is the master swordsman, the man of few words, who pursues the calling of arms for its own sake, seeking no reward other than to participate in the journey and to master his craft to the best of his ability.

Can we do this, you and I, in our endeavor in the arts?

Can we put aside all external or ego-spawned motivations like money, recognition, and so forth?

Can we dance for the dance itself, sing for the song itself, write for the writing itself?

WEEK TWENTY-FOUR

YOU CAN'T BE A PRO
IF YOU CAN'T SAY NO

Day 162
"IT'S ONLY AN HOUR"

"It is only half an hour—It is only an afternoon—It is only an evening," people say to me over and over again; but they don't know that…the mere consciousness of an engagement will sometimes worry a whole day…Whoever is devoted to an art must be content to deliver himself wholly up to it. I am grieved if you suspect me of not wanting to see you, but I can't help it; I must go in my way whether or no.

CHARLES DICKENS, DECLINING AN INVITATION FROM A FRIEND.
BLACK IRISH JAB #5, "LEARNING TO SAY NO"

I'm with you, Charlie! To drag me out from noon to two is to steal my day. I know the person asking doesn't realize this. I know there's no way I can explain it without sounding like a total sonofabitch. But that's the truth.

I'm working! I've got stuff to do. I can't sit around shooting the shit over chips and margaritas. Forget about it.

STEVEN PRESSFIELD

Day 163
AN ASK TOO FAR

Three days ago, I got an e-mail from a guy asking me for thirty free copies of *The War of Art*. There's another person who, because of a colleague-in-common, I've said a courteous no to more than once. He doesn't stop. Each ask is followed by another ask. The most recent was an ask to read his book. "It won't be a problem," he assured me. "It'll only take five hours."

Five hours?

One guy wrote me out of the blue; I did a long interview for him, wrote a foreword for his book and even turned him on to my agent. Finally he started asking for favors for his friends. This was an ask too far. When I said no, he wrote back: "I always knew you were a Hollywood asshole."

Dude! I don't live anywhere near Hollywood.

BLACK IRISH JAB #5, "LEARNING TO SAY NO"

A sociopathic ask is one put forward without a shred of empathy. The asker has no clue that you, the askee, have a life or a family or a career or any demands upon your time. He or she cares only about what you can do for them.

Day 164
"I DON'T TAKE A PISS
WITHOUT GETTING PAID"

"She said everybody else is doing it for nothing. I said everyone else may be an asshole but I'm not. By what right would you call me and ask me to work for nothing? Do you get a paycheck? Does your boss get a paycheck? Would you go to a gas station and ask them to give you free gas? Would you go to the doctor and ask him to take out your spleen for nothing? How dare you call me and ask me to work for nothing! I sell my soul but it's for the highest rate. The highest rate. I don't take a piss without getting paid."

HARLAN ELLISON QUOTED IN BLACK IRISH JAB #5, "LEARNING TO SAY NO"

The passage above comes from one of the all-time great writer's rants—sci-fi legend Harlan Ellison's "Pay the Writer" from *Dreams with Sharp Teeth*. Google it.

It's about R-E-S-P-E-C-T, honey.

STEVEN PRESSFIELD

Day 165
NO MORE MISTER NICE GUY

I just came back from vacation and I'm about to plunge in on a Big New Project.

My first note to myself is, "START SAYING NO."

I hereby vow to stop saying yes to things.

First I'll stop saying yes to things I want to do. My friend Jake, who has tickets to Springsteen? Pass.

I'll go to Lou and Rachel's wedding. I'll be there for the festivities after. But I can't stay out all night, and I won't do anything that'll leave me in no shape to work the next morning.

People are gonna get pissed at me.

I'm sorry.

I'm like the Blues Brothers.

I'm on a mission.

BLACK IRISH JAB #5, "LEARNING TO SAY NO"

Why do I say no? Because I know what it feels like at the end of the day when I've said yes to some bogus "opportunity" because I thought I ought to, or I didn't want to offend someone, or because it seemed like what a Nice Guy would do.

Day 166
CLUELESS ASKS

I turn down all clueless asks. How do I define that term?

1. Anyone who sends me their manuscript unsolicited.

2. Anyone who asks me to meet them for lunch.

3. Anyone who sends me an e-mail headed "Hi" or "Hello there" (or with no salutation at all).

4. Anyone who asks me how to get an agent.

5. Anyone who asks me to introduce them to my agent.

These are not malicious asks. The writers who send them are not bad people. They're just clueless.

BLACK IRISH JAB, #5, "LEARNING TO SAY NO"

Don't ask a writer how to get an agent. Find out yourself.

Don't send an e-mail with an attachment that contains your novel. Are you crazy? Do you think I've got ten (or twenty) free hours to read it?

Do your due diligence. Learn good manners. Find out how the business works.

Day 167
SAYING YES TO "A"
IS SAYING NO TO "B"

The smartest take I've heard on this subject comes from Ken Glickman, in his CD *Time Management*. The key point Ken makes is that when we say yes to one person or activity, we're simultaneously—whether we realize it or not—saying no to another person or activity.

The example Ken gives is if he says yes to a business associate who wants to meet at four on Tuesday, he's saying no to his eight-year-old daughter who has a soccer game at that time and really wants her dad to be there to watch her play.

BLACK IRISH JAB #5, "LEARNING TO SAY NO"

What if we're defending our time to work? Our hour at the gym? What if we just need a nap or twenty minutes to stare out the window?

The elephant in the room is Resistance. Resistance loves "asks"—particularly legitimate, tempting, or well-intentioned ones. Because when we say yes to our friend who wants us to do that benefit program, we're saying no to a day's work.

Day 168
NORMAN MAILER'S REGRETS

The great novelist and nonfiction writer Norman Mailer (*The Naked and the Dead, The Executioner's Song*, many more) was asked toward the end of his life if he had any regrets.

The interviewer expected, I imagine, an answer like, "I wish I'd spent more time with my children or more hours appreciating sunsets."

Instead, Mailer said, "I have three or four more books in my head; I wish I had written them."

BLACK IRISH JAB #5, "LEARNING TO SAY NO"

As writers and artists, you and I live in a different universe from most people. Our interior planets revolve around a singular sun, and that sun is our work. That work takes precedence over everything except kids' soccer games and straight-up emergencies.

STEVEN PRESSFIELD

WEEK TWENTY-FIVE

THE FIGHT

Day 169
"ONLY MEN WHO
DO NOT MIND A HARD LIFE ..."

"Only men who do not mind a hard life, with scanty food, little water and lots of discomfort, men who possess stamina and initiative, need apply."

BRITISH ARMY CIRCULAR (NORTH AFRICA, 1940) SEEKING VOLUNTEERS FOR WHAT WOULD BECOME THE LONG RANGE DESERT GROUP, FROM *KILLING ROMMEL*

They call it adversity because it's adverse.

They call it Resistance because it resists.

Fortunately for you and me, the human being was born for adversity. (The British Army circular above produced more than five thousand applicants.)

It's evolutionary.

It's in our genes.

We love it.

"LIVING THE DREAM, SIR."

A story from the Iraq war. A journalist was passing along the Euphrates in mid-summer, temperature well above 100 degrees. He came upon a lone Marine, deep in a ditch, shoveling. The Marine was in full combat garb—helmet, body armor, the works. The newsman felt for the young man, sweltering and sweating in all that heavy gear. "How's it going, buddy?" he called down.

The Marine looked up with a grin. "Livin' the dream, sir!"

"THE WARRIOR ARCHETYPE", VIDEO SERIES, 2020

Writer, artist, entrepreneur, athlete, mother...we're all peers and equals in the trenches.

Day 171
TRAINING

"The hardship of the exercises is intended less to strengthen the back than to toughen the mind. The Spartans say that any army may win while it still has its legs under it; the real test comes when all strength has fled and the men must produce victory on will alone."

GATES OF FIRE, P. 69

I was cleaning out my garage the other day. I put away four giant boxes, containing the typewritten manuscripts of my first three (unpublished) novels, plus thirty-six screenplays (six months each to write), of which maybe six or seven produced a paycheck while the others never found a buyer or any interest whatsoever.

Training.

It's good for you.

Day 172
HABIT

"Habit will be your champion. When you train the mind to think one way and one way only, when you refuse to allow it to think in another, that will produce great strength in battle."

GATES OF FIRE, P. 139

The choreographer Twyla Tharp starts each day with two hours at the Pumping Iron gym on East Ninety-First Street in Manhattan. My friend Randy Wallace works out with weights underwater in Malibu with Laird Hamilton, the famous big-wave surfer.

Then they go to work.

Twyla and Randy are pursuing fitness only secondarily. What they're really doing is drilling themselves in the habits of a professional.

They are preparing themselves to confront their own Resistance.

Habit is their ally in this daily struggle.

Day 173
ADVERSITY

Because this is war, baby. And war is hell.

THE WAR OF ART, P. 68_

The artist's life can be fun. It can be glamorous; it can be romantic. The days of an entrepreneur or innovator can be packed with excitement and action.

But the inner game is about struggle. We are fighting ourselves and our own tendencies toward self-sabotage every hour, every day. That struggle never goes away and it never gets easier.

This is the life we have chosen, you and I.

It is, by definition, adversity.

STEVEN PRESSFIELD

Day 174
HORSE AND RIDER

"A cavalryman's horse should be smarter than he is. But the horse must never be allowed to know this."

THE VIRTUES OF WAR, P. 183 [HARDBACK]

I actually stole this quote from a book (probably *The Memoirs of Baron de Marbot*, one of my all-time faves) I was using to research cavalry tactics for *The Virtues of War*. I'm not sure what the quip even means.

The closest I can come is this:

We as artists enter battle propelled by our Muse. Yes, she is stronger. Indeed, she is wiser. She is the thunderbolt. We are hanging on for dear life.

But despite it all, you and I must grip the reins with conviction and keep our seat no matter how furiously the creature beneath us gallops or how recklessly she propels us into the melee.

MICKEY AND MOONIE CLIMBING A TREE

I once had two kittens, Mickey and Moonie.

Moonie was the brave one. One day at the base of a pine tree, Moonie started climbing. He extended his little kitten claws and hauled himself, a few inches at a time, up the bark-y barrel of the tree.

What did Mickey do? Did he climb too?

No, he grabbed Moonie by the hind legs and tried to drag him back down.

Mickey wasn't "bad." He was just enacting a natural instinct.

For us as artists, "the fight" is often between our own commitment to achieve and the indifference of others, or even their (conscious or unconscious) sabotage.

WRITING SEMINAR, NASHVILLE, 2019

Gore Vidal is famously quoted as declaring, "Every time a friend succeeds, I die a little."

WEEK TWENTY-SIX

A ROAD MAP OF ACT TWO

Day 176
ACT TWO IS A KILLER

All writers know:

Act One is easy. You come up with some crazy idea and heave it against the wall.

Act Three isn't that hard either. You've figured out where you're going by then. Just tromp on the accelerator and go there.

Ah, but Act Two. Here's David Mamet from *Three Uses of the Knife*.

"A joke from the Algonquin Round Table: A couple of guys are sitting around talking. One says, 'How's the play going?' The other says, 'I'm having second act problems.' Everybody laughs. 'Of *course* you're having second act problems!'"

"WRITING WEDNESDAYS," STEVENPRESSFIELD.COM, 6/9/10

What makes Act Two so hard is it's neither the beginning nor the end. We're out of sight of the shore we left behind, but we haven't yet glimpsed the landfall we're aiming for.

To quote Mamet again, "It's hard to remember that you set out to drain the swamp when you're up to your ass in alligators."

Day 177
THE STAKES INCREASE IN ACT TWO

Marriage Story starts with Nicole and Charlie Barber (Scarlett Johansson and Adam Driver) simply wanting to separate on civil terms.

But by the end of Act Two, Charlie is shouting, "I wish you were dead!" and hiding his face in shame at the words that have just erupted from his mouth.

Each step in this story (consulting an attorney, consulting a second attorney, going before a judge) escalates the stakes for both characters as grimly and as inevitably as the Act Two stages of a murder mystery or a doomsday thriller

This is exactly as it should be.

WRITING SEMINAR, NASHVILLE, 2019

When my own second act starts beating the crap out of me, I sometimes get out the index cards and write one for each scene. I pin them to the wall in sequence and ask myself, "Is each scene escalating the stakes of the story?"

If scene after scene remains at the same level of jeopardy and the same level of consequence, I know I haven't ratcheted up the tension or made the price of failure for my hero(es) higher and more terrifying with each passing beat.

Day 178
OBSTACLES LEAD TO OTHER, GREATER OBSTACLES

Have you watched Aaron Sorkin's Master Class on screenwriting? (I highly recommend it.)

Mr. Sorkin's central concept is the idea of Intention and Obstacle.

The hero has an intention. A series of obstacles impede her or him from achieving this. What she or he does to overcome these obstacles is what produces drama.

"WRITING WEDNESDAYS," STEVENPRESSFIELD.COM, 8/17/18

The essence of Act Two is the hero confronting a twisting, turning sequence of obstacles, each one building on the one before and escalating the tension, the stakes, and the jeopardy.

Day 179
THE VILLAIN IS THE SOURCE
OF THE OBSTACLES THE HERO FACES

The obstacles the hero confronts in Act Two can't arise willy-nilly from everywhere and nowhere. They must originate from a single source—the villain.

One of the great film antagonists is Alain Charnier (Fernando Rey) in William Friedkin's 1971 classic, *The French Connection*. Throughout Act Two this urbane Frenchman and big-time drug smuggler torments the movie's hero, NYPD detective Popeye Doyle (Gene Hackman), relentlessly and exquisitely, always keeping one jump ahead and always making Popeye look like a chump.

Like the zombies in *The Dead Don't Die* or the Tripods in *War of the Worlds*, the villain is the source of all the hero's troubles.

UNPUBLISHED BLACK IRISH JAB, "BAD GUYS, PART FIVE"

When I'm stuck in Act Two, I remind myself, "Go back to the villain. Make him or her smarter, make him/her more formidable, more ruthless, more dangerous."

Day 180
EMOTIONAL DEPTH
INCREASES IN ACT TWO

In Act Two the obstacles the hero faces must escalate not just quantitively but qualitatively.

UNPUBLISHED BLACK IRISH JAB, "BAD GUYS, PART FIVE"

The mission of Captain Willard (Martin Sheen) in *Apocalypse Now* starts out as one of simple assassination. "Go upriver, kill evil Colonel Kurtz (Marlon Brando), return to receive the praise of a grateful nation."

But as Willard advances through obstacle after obstacle on his riverine odyssey, his perspective on the mission deepens. Willard comes face to face with the moral dilemma of the Vietnam War itself, not only in the context of this current American intervention, but in all this troubled land's past (and all the wars of all mankind's past) back to the savage heart—Conrad's *Heart of Darkness*—of the human race itself.

Day 181
EMOTIONAL DEPTH
INCREASES ON-THEME IN ACT TWO

Silver Linings Playbook is about nuttiness, specifically the garden-variety OCD-ness that gets in the way of love. Here's our hero Tiffany (Jennifer Lawrence) proving to her boyfriend's father Pat, Sr. (Robert De Niro) that she is not bad luck for Pat, Jr. (Bradley Cooper)—and not the cause of Pat, Sr.'s beloved Philadelphia Eagles losing.

> TIFFANY
>
> The first night that Pat and I met at my
> sister's, the Eagles beat the 49ers handily,
> forty to twenty-six. The next time we went
> for a run the Eagles beat the Falcons, twen-
> ty-seven to fourteen. The third time we got
> together we had Raisin Bran in the diner
> and the Phillies dominated Tampa Bay in
> the fourth game of the World Series, ten
> to two.
>
> PAT, SR.
>
> Let me think about that. Wait a minute.

UNPUBLISHED "WRITING WEDNESDAYS"

If you're gonna fight crazy, you gotta fight by crazy's rules. Emotional depth increases on-theme.

Day 182
ACT TWO OF OUR REAL LIVES

For you and me, Act Two of our real lives is the passage we live out before we commit heart-and-soul to our artistic or moral or entrepreneurial calling.

Like the heroes of our stories, we're lost. Like our heroes, we're searching. Like our heroes we reach a point where we hit the wall. Where we, as anchorman Howard Beale (Peter Finch) declared of himself in Paddy Chayefsky's *Network*, "run out of bullshit."

WRITING SEMINAR, NASHVILLE, 2019

We'll be getting, in these pages, to the concept of the All Is Lost Moment.

When you hit that yourself, you'll know it.

WEEK TWENTY-SEVEN

THE HERO IN ACT TWO

THE DIFFERENCE BETWEEN HEROES AND VILLAINS

What separates the Good Guy from the Bad Guy is the Good Guy is capable of sacrificing himself (or his happiness or future) for the good of others.

"WRITING WEDNESDAYS," STEVENPRESSFIELD.COM, 11/22/17

Here's an exception, from 1939's *Gunga Din*. The ostensible villain is "the Guru" of the Strangler Cult (Eduardo Ciannelli). In his ultimate scene the Guru is trapped in the evil tower with no chance of escape. What does he do? He steps to the brink of a pit seething with poisonous vipers.

"You have sworn to give your lives, if necessary for your country, which is England. Well, India is my country, and I can die for it as readily as you can for yours."

And he leaps into the pit.

Which makes us think, "Hmm, maybe the Guru is not the villain after all. Could the villain instead be England's unjust colonial domination of India?"

Day 184
WHEN THE VILLAIN ACTS LIKE A HERO

Another seeming villain who sacrifices himself is Roy Batty (Rutger Hauer), the replicant leader in the 1978 *Blade Runner*. Roy's choice in the climax is to save the man who is trying to kill him, Blade Runner Rick Deckard (Harrison Ford), while he himself expires as his programmed lifespan runs out.

> ROY BATTY
> I've seen things you people wouldn't believe.
> Attack ships on fire off the shoulder of Orion.
> I've watched C-beams glitter in the dark near
> the Tannhäuser Gate. All those moments will
> be lost in time, like tears in rain. Time to die.

"WRITING WEDNESDAYS", STEVENPRESSFIELD.COM, 11/22/17

By sacrificing himself and saving Deckard, Roy Batty goes from a villain of the larger piece (he has indeed murdered a few people) to the hero of the Batty-Deckard subplot.

Day 185
THE HERO IS
CAPABLE OF SELF-SACRIFICE

The preceding two exceptions aside, it can be pretty safely said that *the villain is not capable of self-sacrifice while the hero is.*

The Seven Samurai are willing to give their lives for the villagers.

Clarice Starling enters serial killer Buffalo Bill's den in pitch blackness to save the murderer's captive, Catherine Martin.

Sydney Carton willingly takes Edward Darnay's place beneath the guillotine in *A Tale of Two Cities.*

Those are heroes.

The hero is capable of the ultimate sacrifice.

UNPUBLISHED BLACK IRISH JAB, "HEROES AND VILLAINS"

But the hero must not throw away her life (or her happiness or cherished dream or her future) willy-nilly. The act must be taken for the good of another or for the greater good of the community—local or global or cosmic.

I was watching the movie *Logan* on TV last night. Do you know it? It's one of the X-Men flicks, starring Hugh Jackman as "the Wolverine," Though in this story he's the more human-ish version of that character, called "Logan."

Clearly, Logan is crafted in the tradition of male/adventure leads— Bogart in *Casablanca*, Harrison Ford in *Star Wars*, Clint Eastwood in anything. He starts off crusty and uncaring, spouting lines like, "Leave me alone, I can't help you" or "It's none of my business! Get away from me!"

But what happens through Act Two?

Logan changes.

"WRITING WEDNESDAYS," STEVENPRESSFIELD.COM, 6/19/19

The writers (Scott Frank & James Mangold and Michael Green) move Logan, increment by increment, from a bitter, self-despairing character to a hero, i.e., a human being capable of sacrificing himself for the good of others.

I won't ruin the ending for you if you haven't seen *Logan*. Suffice it to say that you and I must do the same for our protagonist through Act Two and into Act Three.

Day 187
GIVE YOUR HERO A HERO SPEECH

One of my faves comes from the movie *Fury*, the Brad Pitt-starrer about a lone American tank driving deep into Nazi Germany in the closing weeks of WWII. The crisis comes when the tank hits a land mine and becomes incapacitated just as a battalion of SS infantry is tramping down the road in its direction.

The tank crew decides to stay. They "button up" the hatches and make ready to stand and die.

Director-writer David Ayer gives the Hero Speech to the tank's gunner, Boyd "Bible" Swan, played by Shia LaBeouf.

> SWAN
>
> There's a Bible verse I think about some-
> times. Many times. It goes, "And I heard the
> voice of the Lord saying, 'Who shall I send,
> and who will go for us?' Then I said, 'Here
> am I. Send me.'"

BLACK IRISH JAB #16, "BAD GUYS, PART THREE"

The hero's ultimate hour of choice comes in the climax, in Act Three. But we, the writers, must set this moment up emotionally and narratively—scene by scene, increment by increment—throughout Act Two.

One of the great hero speeches comes from Ron Shelton's *Bull Durham.*

Nuke LaLoosh (Tim Robbins), the clueless but athletically gifted pitcher, has just been called up from the minor leagues to the majors. Crash Davis (Kevin Costner), the veteran catcher who has been mentoring Nuke, has just heard the news. Crash knows that he himself will never get that life-changing call, even though he's ten times smarter than Nuke and has worked ten times harder.

> CRASH DAVIS
> Know what the difference between hitting
> .250 and .300 is? It's 25 hits. 25 hits in 500
> at bats is 50 points, okay? That means if
> you get just one extra flare a week—just
> one—you get a groundball, you get a
> groundball with eyes...you get a dying quail,
> just one more dying quail a week...and
> you're in Yankee Stadium.

BLACK IRISH JAB #16, "BAD GUYS, PART THREE"

Is this speech a lament? No. It's an epiphany. It's Crash facing a terrible truth, one he has avoided his whole life. It's Crash changing.

Day 189
THE SHORTEST (AND MAYBE GREATEST) HERO SPEECH EVER

Mexico, 1913. The surviving members of the outlaw band known as the Wild Bunch (William Holden, Ernest Borgnine, Ben Johnson, and Warren Oates) have seen their companion Angel (Jaime Sanchez) captured and tortured by the evil generalissimo Mapache and been unable to rescue him because of the overwhelming numbers of Mapache's soldiers.

The Bunch passes a guilt-ravaged night in the village where Mapache and his troops (and Angel, still in captivity) have laid up. Waking in the morning, William Holden, the leader of the Bunch, straps on his gun and steps into the doorway of the room where his compadres Ben Johnson and Warren Oates are just groaning awake.

Holden meets Oates' eye and says simply, "Let's go."

In the audience we know Holden means, "Let's take on Mapache's army in the cause of rescuing Angel...and give our lives in the process."

Oates responds, "Why not?"

BLACK IRISH JAB #16, "BAD GUYS, PART THREE"

I watch Sam Peckinpah's *The Wild Bunch* once a year at least, just to remind myself what great storytelling and filmmaking is all about.

WEEK TWENTY-EIGHT

THE HERO'S JOURNEY
IN OUR REAL LIVES

Day 190
THE MYTHS AND YOU AND ME

The word "hero" must be taken with a grain of salt when we speak of the hero's journey, either in our stories or in our real lives. Most of the time, the "hero" is lost, disoriented, stumbling and bumbling. If you don't believe me, study the myths.

Jason and his Argonauts were all screwed up. So were Theseus and Hercules and Perseus and Odysseus, not to mention Arjuna, St. George and Quetzalcoatl. David Mamet writes in *Three Uses of the Knife:*

"In his analysis of world myth, Joseph Campbell calls this period *in the belly of the beast*—the time, which is not the beginning and not the end, the time when the artist and the protagonist doubt themselves and wish the journey had never begun."

"THE WARRIOR ARCHETYPE" INSTAGRAM SERIES, 2020

Remember, we're speaking of the hero's journey not only as a template for the stories we write but also as the pattern we find ourselves living out in our real and artistic lives.

What, then, are the characteristics of the hero's journey?

Day 191
THE HERO'S JOURNEY LIES DORMANT

The template for the hero's journey lies dormant in our psyches for years and then kicks in with irresistible power precisely at the time it is needed. The Call, as Joseph Campbell termed it, seizes its owner with a passionate urgency to act out, in real life, a journey to what Jung called "individuation," even though the recipient of the Call is completely oblivious of the journey's imperative.

WRITING SEMINAR, NASHVILLE, 2019

The hero's journey is the passage to becoming an artist, a mother, a warrior, an entrepreneur, a grownup.

It's the passage to becoming an individual, to becoming ourselves.

Day 192
THE HERO'S JOURNEY IS INTERNAL

The hero's journey, as you and I live it out in our real lives, takes place inside our skulls.

The real people we encounter and clash with and love, and the real events we endure or undergo or experience—though each possesses its own soul and its own reality and is, in truth, upon its own hero's journey—are for us but avatars in the drama that is playing out upon the deepest levels of our psyches.

WRITING SEMINAR, NASHVILLE, 2019

You can live out the hero's journey in a cubicle or in a prison cell. It can happen inside you-the-drug-addict, you-the-drunk, you-the-wife-beater or you-the-beaten-wife. Or it can go the other way. You can be a superstar, a captain of industry. You can be Mother Teresa.

Day 193
THE HERO'S JOURNEY IS SACRED

Though its external manifestation may appear as pointless, foolish, preposterous, even excruciating (or boring and mundane) from the outside, the hero's journey remains pure and holy within.

WRITING SEMINAR, NASHVILLE, 2019

The template of the hero's journey is ancient and honorable. No matter how clumsily we stumble along the path, our steps remain consecrated because they carry us back to ourselves.

The only crime we can commit on the hero's journey is to stop before we reach the end.

Day 194
THE HERO'S JOURNEY IS ENACTED IN A BENIGHTED STATE

We, the heroes on our journey, are blind. We're acting out. We're clueless.

We're trying to ascend to consciousness. But within the maelstrom, we're so oblivious and so overwhelmed we don't even know we're trying. We don't know anything, except that we are on Mr. Toad's Wild Ride and we can't get off.

WRITING SEMINAR, NASHVILLE, 2019

A defining characteristic of the hero's journey is that the hero has no idea he or she is on the hero's journey.

Day 195
THE HERO'S JOURNEY
IS MANDATORY

You can catch the ride early or catch it late. But, like it or not, you were born with your ticket.

Sooner or later, the conductor will call, "All Aboard!" and the train—with you on it—will pull out of the station.

WRITING SEMINAR, NASHVILLE, 2019

And that's just one hero's journey. For most of us, there are many—hero's journeys within hero's journeys.

Day 196
THE HERO'S JOURNEY IS NOT SOLITARY

In *The Legend of Bagger Vance* I wrote not of a solitary protagonist but of a constellation of kindred souls, who travel together through life after life in a defined and structured relationship to one another, even though they possess no memory of this formation from one lifetime to the next and have to discover it anew (or fail to discover it) with each successive incarnation.

I believe in that reality to this day.

UNPUBLISHED BLACK IRISH JAB, "THE HERO'S JOURNEY"

The souls we encounter on our hero's journey do not appear randomly. We call them forth by some alchemy that can't be proven but can be felt.

Why do our foes and nemeses feel so familiar? Why, when we love, do we often experience the communion as something we have felt and known in the past?

I don't know, but I believe it's true. We are not alone on our hero's journey, any more than were Frodo or Dorothy or Alice Through the Looking Glass.

WEEK TWENTY-NINE

MAKE YOUR HERO SUFFER

Day 197
GIVE YOUR HERO A TORTURE SCENE

We were writing *Above the Law* when one of the *Lethal Weapon* movies (I forget which) came out. In it was a scene where the hero, played by Mel Gibson, was tortured by the villain. Steven Seagal saw the movie. He came in the next day on fire.

"Write me a scene where I get tortured."

My first thought was, "That is the dumbest, most derivative idea I've ever heard."

But Steve was right.

A scene of that type is a convention of the thriller genre, what Shawn Coyne calls the Hero at the Mercy of the Villain Scene.

We gave Steve a torture scene and it played like gangbusters.

"WRITING WEDNESDAYS," STEVENPRESSFIELD.COM, 1/6/16

We as writers are on our own hero's journey, which involves ordeals, initiations, torments, agony, and all kinds of nasty stuff. But don't forget, the protagonists in our stories are on their journeys as well.

They need to suffer too.

It's our job to make them suffer.

As writers, you and I may sometimes be tempted to go easy on our protagonists. After all, we like them. We're rooting for them. Sometimes they're even thinly veiled versions of ourselves.

But giving our heroes a break is the worst thing we can do.

Instead, pour on the misery.

Beat them up like Gus Fring did to Walter White and Jesse Pinkman in *Breaking Bad* or Gene Hackman did to Clint Eastwood (not to mention Morgan Freeman) in *Unforgiven*. Torture them emotionally like Julianne Moore was tortured in *Far from Heaven* and *Still Alice*. Break their hearts like Meryl Streep in *Out of Africa* (or any, or all, of Ms. Streep's movies.)

Readers will love it.

Audiences will love it.

BLACK IRISH JAB #9, "MAKE YOUR HERO SUFFER"

Think of the protagonist in your novel as if he or she were an actor in a motion picture. Actors love to suffer. They win Oscars for suffering. Renee Zellweger in *Judy*. Daniel Day-Lewis in *My Left Foot*. Frances McDormand in *Nomadland*.

Day 199
THE MORE THE HERO SUFFERS, THE BETTER

We learn from stories. We learn about life.

That's why the hero must suffer.

We the readers, the moviegoers, don't want a shallow vicarious experience. We want our detective, our prize fighter, our desperate housewife to push his or her drama to the limit. The stakes in every great story are life and death, or worse. Remember what Edward G. Robinson as Barton Keyes declared (thank you, Billy Wilder) in *Double Indemnity*:

> BARTON KEYES
> They're stuck with each other and they gotta
> ride all the way to the end of the line and it's a
> one-way trip and the last stop is the cemetery.

UNPUBLISHED BLACK IRISH JAB, "MAKE YOUR HERO SUFFER, PART TWO"

The hero is us. We're living his or her life, and we want to live it to the last breath and the final drop of blood.

Extreme happiness plays great for a few moments. But extreme suffering, as long as its forms keep changing, is always interesting.

Day 200
WHY IS THE HERO'S SUFFERING
SO IMPORTANT?

Why, we might ask, does the hero have to suffer at all? Why can't she just be happy? Wouldn't that work just as well in a story?

Answer: No.

The hero has to suffer because suffering produces insight.

Suffering leads to wisdom.

Suffering forces the hero to change.

BLACK IRISH JAB #9, "MAKE YOUR HERO SUFFER"

Raskolnikov changes in *Crime and Punishment*. The unnamed narrator in Knut Hamsun's *Hunger* changes. Stephen Hawking (Eddie Redmayne) changes in *The Theory of Everything*. Each one traverses a hero's journey. Each one encounters obstacles. Each one must dig deep within themselves in order to overcome (or fail to overcome) these obstacles.

Each one suffers thereby. Each one learns. Each one's character becomes revealed.

And each one is altered, for good or ill, by his or her suffering.

Day 201
SUFFERING = INSIGHT = CHANGE

You, the writer, invent your hero's suffering in order to make her change.

What ordeal, you ask yourself, can I put my protagonist through that will compel her to deepen her understanding of life and of herself, that will force her to confront some issue she has either been oblivious to or deliberately hiding from, that will make her change and grow (even if that change and growth involve further suffering)?

You ask yourself that because if you didn't ask it, there would be no story.

BLACK IRISH JAB #9, "MAKE YOUR HERO SUFFER"

We as writers must also ask, "What *kind of suffering* should our hero undergo?"

THE HERO'S SUFFERING
MUST BE ON-THEME

The theme of *Cool Hand Luke* is authority and the individual's response to it—specifically the authority of society imposed upon its members by force.

Here's the Prison Captain, played by Strother Martin, explaining to his inmates how the system works.

> PRISON CAPTAIN
> You run one time, you got yourself one set
> of chains. You run twice, you got yourself
> two sets. You ain't gonna need no third set,
> 'cause you gonna get your mind right.

Every instance of suffering inflicted upon Luke (Paul Newman) by the captain and his brutal "bosses" arises directly from this theme, this issue that the film is built around and upon.

BLACK IRISH JAB #9, "MAKE YOUR HERO SUFFER"

As writers, we can't simply pile agonies willy-nilly upon our protagonists (though that will work too).

Their ordeal has to be focused.

It must be on-theme.

Day 203
MAKE YOUR HERO FIGHT THROUGH HER SUFFERING

It's not enough that our hero endure suffering. He must fight through it.

Otherwise we have no story.

Otherwise we have no hero.

BLACK IRISH JAB #9, "MAKE YOUR HERO SUFFER"

The suffering of the hero on her journey is not mute endurance but the overcoming of a series of trials. It's an initiation into a deeper understanding of life.

The hero doesn't need to win every battle. She doesn't need to win any of them. But she has to fight. She has to learn.

Julianne Moore's character in *Far from Heaven* loses every battle. Same with Alan Ladd in *Shane*. Even Bogey in *Casablanca* loses (or, more accurately, sacrifices) everything—his night club, the woman he loves, even his fashionable hard-boiled attitude. But he becomes his deeper, nobler self.

What produces the changes in all these characters is suffering.

WEEK THIRTY

FURTHER CHARACTERISTICS
OF THE HERO'S JOURNEY

THE HERO'S JOURNEY IS A DEBACLE

Though the term "hero's journey" sounds noble and romantic, in the event it's usually a calamity. We're careening through a maze that's simultaneously flooded and on fire, crashing blindly into flaming wall after flaming wall.

The good news is we're learning.

We're learning the maze.

We're learning that we ourselves, consciously or unconsciously, are and have been willing accomplices to these crimes against ourselves and our soul-integrity.

And we're learning that we don't want to do this shit ever again.

UNPUBLISHED BLACK IRISH JAB, "THE HERO'S JOURNEY"

This principle is a corollary to "Make Your Hero Suffer."

Serve up some serious torment for your protagonist.

Why should she have it any easier than you and I do in our real lives?

Day 205
THE MORE EXCRUCIATING
THE HERO'S JOURNEY, THE BETTER

What we don't want at this stage of our evolution/story is the Hero's Journey Lite.

We want the adult portion.

We want the full catastrophe.

Why? Because the full catastrophe sticks. The full catastrophe tattoos itself on our brain (and our hero's) so we never forget.

UNPUBLISHED BLACK IRISH JAB, "THE HERO'S JOURNEY"

Rule of thumb for fiction writers: The more agony you can put your protagonist through, the more the audience will love it.

Not because we as readers are rooting against our hero. We're not. We're rooting for him. We just know in our guts that the more we suffer (or the more our fictional heroes do), the deeper the lessons will sink in and the better we (and they) will be in the end.

One proviso of course: We have to survive the journey.

Day 206
THE HERO'S JOURNEY IS KINDA FUN

No one is born a pro. You've got to fall before you hit bottom, and sometimes that fall can be a hell of a ride.

So here's to blackouts and divorces, to lost jobs and lost cash and lost self-respect. Here's to time on the street. Here's to years we can't remember. Here's to bad friends and cheating spouses—and to us, too, for being at times both.

TURNING PRO, P. 16

As excruciating as we choose to make Act Two for our heroes, it should also be fun.

Did you ever see the English movie *Withnail and I*, written and directed by Bruce Robinson, based on his own crazy life in London during the late 1960s?

The two eponymous friends, played by Richard E. Grant and Paul McGann, part at the end, never to see each other again (we assume). But the intensity of their shared journey has made them closer than brothers, and each has stamped his impress on the other more profoundly than any other, before or since.

THE HERO'S JOURNEY IS DEMOCRATIC

All heroes' journeys are created equal. Mine is no better than yours, and yours is in no way superior to mine.

Einstein's Special Theory of Relativity states that every point in the universe is of equal value, physically and mathematically. Is our spaceship passing Planet Nine or is Planet Nine passing us?

UNPUBLISHED BLACK IRISH JAB, "THE HERO'S JOURNEY"

In other words, you and I and the homecoming queen and the Delta Force commando are the same. No one's journey is more valid than anyone else's. Each will play out against its own mythological backdrop, and each will be just what the doctor ordered.

Day 208
THE HERO'S JOURNEY
IS A PRODUCT OF RESISTANCE

Before the journey, the hero is mired in Resistance. He's stuck. He's going nowhere. Like Luke Skywalker repairing binary evaporators on Uncle Owen and Aunt Beru's moisture farm on the planet Tatooine, he is miserable, marooned, pissed off. He feels like he's dying. If he stays where he is, he will die.

UNPUBLISHED BLACK IRISH JAB, "THE HERO'S JOURNEY"

Maybe the Call takes the form of an external event. The unnamed narrator (Edward Norton) meets Tyler Durden (Brad Pitt) in *Fight Club*. Jack Ryan (Alec Baldwin) stumbles upon the silent "caterpillar drive" in *The Hunt for Red October*.

More often the Call comes from within. Some seismic shift occurs far below the level of consciousness, and this shift creates a pressure that impels us out of our pre-journey Ordinary World.

STEVEN PRESSFIELD

Day 209
THE HERO'S JOURNEY
PRODUCES FEAR

The hero feels a call inside her. The call is centered in her heart and her belly. She feels it physically.

The call is the future, her Self-to-be. What's calling her is who she must and will become.

The hero is scared. She doesn't feel like a hero. She feels like a loser.

UNPUBLISHED BLACK IRISH JAB, "THE HERO'S JOURNEY"

Resistance's primary form of manifestation is fear. That's what the hero feels now. She can't complete her dissertation; can't take the mike at the comedy club; can't quit her job at the Cosmodemonic Telegraph Company.

Sometimes the hero has to manufacture a break to overcome this fear. Sometimes the break appears all by itself. No matter. Critical mass has been reached. Our hero's life has exploded.

The journey has begun.

THE HERO'S JOURNEY IS IRRETRIEVABLE

Once the young James Tiberius Kirk (Chris Pine) enters Starfleet Academy, he can never turn back. Once Chris Washington in *Get Out* (Daniel Kaluuya) heads off for a weekend at his girlfriend's parents' country place, the die has been cast.

There are no do-overs on the hero's journey and no takebacks.

You (and your hero) are on your way.

UNPUBLISHED BLACK IRISH JAB, "THE HERO'S JOURNEY"

The Act One Curtain represents the point of no return for our hero on his journey. He has crossed the Rubicon. Resolution is no longer possible except by continuing all the way to the end of the line.

WEEK THIRTY-ONE

A ROAD MAP
OF ACT TWO, PART TWO

Day 211
ACT TWO BUILDS TO A MIDPOINT

"There are two halves to a movie script and the midpoint...is the threshold between them. We can talk about the importance of the two act breaks, but to me the midpoint is as important, especially in the early going to laying out a script's beats."

This is Blake Snyder from *Save the Cat!*, page 82. What he states about movies is equally applicable to novels and dramas, not to say nonfiction, including TED talks and children's books.

UNPUBLISHED BLACK IRISH JAB, "ACT TWO HORRORS"

Are you struggling in your Act Two? (Silly question.)

One exercise that may help break the logjam is to ask, "Where is my midpoint? What spot divides the story into two halves?"

Does *something big* happen there? Does the story "turn"? Are the stakes raised dramatically?

I have found myself at this hellish junction many times. Focusing on the midpoint helps.

THE STAKES ARE RAISED
AT THE MIDPOINT

Every great second act has a midpoint. In this instant something happens that ratchets our story to a higher level. The stakes go up, way up.

> MICHAEL CORLEONE
> They want to have a meeting with me.
> Right? It'll be me, McCluskey and Sollozzo.
> Let's set the meeting. Get our informers to
> find out where it's going to be held. Now we
> insist it's a public place, a bar, a restaurant,
> some place where there's people so I feel
> safe. They're going to search me when I first
> meet them. Right? So I can't have a weap-
> on on me then. But if Clemenza can figure
> a way to have a weapon planted there for
> me...then I'll kill them both.

"WRITING WEDNESDAYS", WWW.STEVENPRESSFIELD.COM, 1/29/20

This speech from Michael Corleone (Al Pacino) changes everything in *The Godfather*.

Day 213
MICHAEL'S MOMENT, CONTINUED

Consider what happens in the Midpoint Scene cited yesterday.

Up to this juncture in *The Godfather*, Michael has been at best a minor player. His older brother Sonny and the capos Tessio and Clemenza have tried to protect him and keep him out of the emergency that is engulfing the Corleone family. At this point in the story, Michael is still in essence a civilian—a Marine Corps captain freshly home from WWII, with an innocent, non-family fiancée with whom he intends to make a life outside of the Mob and its business.

That's how we—and all the characters in the movie—perceive Michael at the start of this Midpoint Scene.

By its finish, ninety seconds later, every assumption has been overturned. We realize Michael is the hero of this drama. *The Godfather* is his story, not the Don's. And he will turn out to be the rightful and only possible heir to his father's empire.

"WRITING WEDNESDAYS," STEVENPRESSFIELD.COM, 1/29/20

A great story has a sense of narrative inevitability. The midpoint of Act Two is when that inevitability displays itself in high relief.

THE MIDPOINT OF
LAWRENCE OF ARABIA

Luckily for us, *Lawrence of Arabia* has an intermission. So we get to see exactly where director David Lean thought the midpoint of his story fell.

In the penultimate scene before intermission, Lawrence learns from his superiors, General Allenby and the diplomat Dryden, that England and France have concluded a secret agreement to divide the Ottoman Empire (including Arabia) between them after the war. This pact, the true historical Sykes-Picot Agreement, is a monumental betrayal of every promise Lawrence has made to his friends, Prince Feisal and his Bedouin warriors.

Yet Lawrence goes along with this, saying nothing to Feisal and the Arabs, hoping (we imagine) that he can somehow, in the climactic battles to come, overturn events by sheer force of brilliance and audacity.

UNPUBLISHED "WRITING WEDNESDAY", STEVENPRESSFIELD.COM

Stakes? Way up. Hero's choice? Fatal. Bottom line: Exactly what we as storytellers want in a midpoint.

Day 215
THE HERO TAKES SIDES
AT THE MIDPOINT

Michael Corleone, when he says in the midpoint scene, "… then I'll kill them both," has made a choice that will define his life from this moment to the grave. He has taken sides in the most fatal sense. He has declared, "I am with the family. The family supersedes everything."

"WRITING WEDNESDAYS," STEVENPRESSFIELD.COM, 1/29/20

When you and I analyze the Act Two Midpoint in our own novel or screenplay, we must ask ourselves: "Does this moment represent an irretrievable choice for our protagonist? Has our hero taken sides via a decision she cannot take back?"

WALTER SOBCHAK (JOHN GOODMAN)
You want a toe? I can get you a toe, Dude.
There are ways. You don't wanna know
about it, believe me.

The midpoint of *The Big Lebowski* comes when the secondary Bad Guys, the Nihilists who have kidnapped Bunny Lebowski, deliver to her husband, the Big Lebowski, a severed female toe with red nail polish on it and, threatening to murder Bunny, escalate their demands for ransom.

When our hero, the Dude, learns this, he changes just as dramatically as Michael Corleone in *The Godfather*.

Before, the Dude had only wanted to get his carpet back.

Now he wants to save Bunny, to get to the bottom of this case, and to hold whoever is behind all this craziness accountable.

UNPUBLISHED BLACK IRISH JAB, "DUDEOLOGY, PART TWO"

Even through a haze of White Russians and doobie smoke, our champion reveals himself to be a good man with a sense of responsibility to others.

He's a hero.

He changes.

Day 217
THE HERO'S IDENTITY
CHANGES AT THE MIDPOINT

Lieutenant John Dunbar (Kevin Costner) "turns Injun" at the midpoint of *Dances with Wolves*. He takes sides.

He has ceased being "Lieutenant Dunbar."

He has become "Dances with Wolves."

With this, our hero's "want" changes too. It goes from some obscure notion of "completing his mission" as an army officer to the passionate commitment to defend the Lakota Sioux people from the approaching onslaught of white settlers, backed by the might of the US military and the government in Washington, DC.

Dunbar no longer holds any intention of returning to the "real world." He is committed to his new life, his new identity, and his new tribe.

UNPUBLISHED BLACK IRISH JAB, "ANATOMY OF ACT TWO"

Again, stakes way up.

Hero's choice: fatal.

Hero's commitment: irreversible.

WEEK THIRTY-TWO

SECOND ACT HORRORS

Day 218
WELCOME TO HELL

Why have we gone into such excruciating detail over the past few [weeks] (with more still to come) over the structure and composition of Act Two?

Because inevitably in this middle passage, the entire edifice of our novel, our screenplay, our videogame will come crashing down.

DO THE WORK, P. 58

Now is when we need that road map. Now is when we need a good stiff drink.

So let's rally.

Let's ask ourselves what went wrong and how we can make it right again.

Day 219
THE BIG CRASH

We were going so great. Our project was in high gear. We felt as if we were (almost) past the Freak-Out point.

Then, inevitably…everything crashes.

If we're producing a movie, the star checks into rehab. If it's a business venture, the bank pulls our funding. If it's you and me as writers, we hit the wall of Act Two.

The Big Crash is so predictable, across all fields of enterprise, that we can practically set our watches by it.

Bank on it. It's gonna happen.

DO THE WORK, P. 72

Remember when we were talking earlier about the hero's journey? The monsters and the villains and the shapeshifters who would come forward to block our real-life passage, as they did to Theseus and Jason and Bellerophon, not to mention Batman, Superman, and the Wolverine?

Well, that's what's happening now, here in the bowels of Act Two.

Day 220
THE BIG CRASH
COMES OUT OF NOWHERE

The worst part of the Big Crash is that nothing can prepare us for it. Why? Because the crash arises organically, spawned by some act of commission or omission that we ourselves took or countenanced back at the project's inception.

DO THE WORK, P. 72

Blind spots.

We thought we had our story figured out.

We imagined the pieces all fit together, that the rockets ignited at Zero Minus Zero and the whole grand show blasted into the stratosphere.

It didn't.

WTF do we do now?

Day 221
MY OWN BIGGEST CRASH

Five years ago, I had an idea for a new novel, *36 Righteous Men*. I did what I always do: I put the piece together in abbreviated form and sent it to my editor and business partner Shawn Coyne.

He loved it.

I plunged in.

Cut to fifteen months later. I sent the finished manuscript (Draft #10) to Shawn.

He hated it.

"WRITING WEDNESDAYS," STEVENPRESSFIELD.COM, 7/5/17

The implosion of a book-in-progress may be a small thing in the overall scheme of world affairs. But to the writer—to you and me—a go-back-to-Square-One diagnosis from a pro we trust hits us like a kick in the guts.

Did I freak out?

Hell yes.

Did I lose my shit?

Big time.

Day 222
THE BIG CRASH (OFTEN) COMES
AFTER WE'VE FINISHED

Your book/movie/start-up is a wrap. You're almost ready to ship it (in Seth Godin's spot-on phrase) to the wide world. But first, just to be sure it's ready, you expose it to feedback from close compadres you trust.

It gets slammed.

What, one might ask, does this have to do with Act Two (which is, after all, the subject we've been focusing on in these pages for the past few months)?

Answer: the problem is *always* in Act Two.

The "middle passage" is universally where we lost our way.

WRITING SEMINAR, NASHVILLE, 2019

When our Second Act works, Act Three becomes a straight-up dash to the finish line. All we have to do is tromp the accelerator and race to the checkered flag.

But when Act Two is out of whack, we highball into the final straightaway with smoke pouring from our manifold, flames blasting from our exhaust, and the steering wheel shimmying like Sister Kate.

Day 223
RESISTANCE AT THE PHD LEVEL

The plot so far:

April 28, 2017. Shawn sends me his editorial notes on my new manuscript (Draft #10). Same day: I go into shock.

Two weeks later: I summon the courage to read Shawn's notes again. I succumb to shock a second time.

For sure I am going through the Kubler-Ross stages of grief: denial, anger, bargaining, depression. The objective is to get to the final stage—acceptance.

Acceptance meaning the ability to read Shawn's notes objectively (or as objectively as possible) and respond to them like a professional, i.e., without ego, without defensiveness, without laziness or short-cut-itis.

BLACK IRISH JAB #12, "STARTING OVER, PART ONE"

Reading Shawn's notes for the first, and even the second time, I literally *cannot understand them*. Yet I know, in some hazy part of my brain, Shawn's notes are right.

Problem: How do I come back from the fetal position and shake off that defensive armor of self-protection?

Day 224
PROFESSIONALS AND AMATEURS

Are we dwelling too long on the hell of Act Two? Stick with me. This passage is what separates the real writers (and artists and entrepreneurs) from the wannabes.

"How many times [writes David Mamet in *Three Uses of the Knife*] have we heard (and said): Yes, I know I was cautioned that the way would become difficult and I would want to quit, that such was inevitable, and that at exactly this point the battle would be lost or won. Yes, I know all that, but those who cautioned me could not have foreseen the magnitude of the specific difficulties I am encountering at this point—difficulties, which must, sadly, but I have no choice, force me to resign the struggle (and have a drink, a cigarette, an affair, a rest), in short, to declare failure."

UNPUBLISHED BLACK IRISH JAB, "SECOND ACT HORRORS"

I was reading Mamet's *Three Uses of the Knife* at the exact time I was struggling with Act Two of *36 Righteous Men*. When I came to the passage above, it was all I could do to keep from weeping.

The answer that saved me?

"Go back to genre."

WEEK THIRTY-THREE

GO BACK TO GENRE

Day 225
WHAT IS GENRE?

In my screenwriting days, when my writing partner Stanley and I were searching for a new idea, the first question we'd ask ourselves was, "What kind of movie do *we ourselves* want to see?"

Do we wanna see a thriller? A love story? An apocalyptic zombie saga?

In other words, we were debating genre.

What genre would be fun to write in? What genre is hot right now at the box office? What genres should we definitely stay away from?

NOBODY WANTS TO READ YOUR SH*T, P. 62

Genre may be the most important single factor, from a writer's point of view, both in crafting the work and in attempting to find a market for it.

Why?

Because every film (and novel and play, not to mention dance, nonprofit, and TED talk) falls into a genre, and every genre has its own ironclad, unbreakable principles of structure and composition.

STEVEN PRESSFIELD

Day 226
GENRE GETS A BAD RAP

I remember when *Above the Law* got reviewed in *Daily Variety*. The paper gave the film's title and then, right after that, wrote "Exploitation."

In other words, that was the genre *Variety* had assigned to it.

I was outraged. "How about 'cop thriller'? What's wrong with 'detective story'? I'll even vote for 'redemption saga'!"

UNPUBLISHED BLACK IRISH JAB, "GO BACK TO GENRE"

To call a movie a "genre film" is an insult. The term implies a slavish adherence to formula, devoid of originality or creativity.

But every book is a genre book, and every motion picture is a genre film. What's wrong with that?

Romeo and Juliet is a love story. That's a genre.

The *Odyssey* is a hero's journey saga. That's a genre.

Even the Bible falls into a genre, and if you don't believe me, ask Cecil B. DeMille.

Day 227
EVERY GENRE HAS CONVENTIONS

Beating up the hero always works. *Cool Hand Luke*. *The Grapes of Wrath*. Every James Bond movie.

If our Western has two gunslingers, they have to shoot it out in the final reel. If our Love Story features a pair of lovers, the two must move apart in the story's middle before they come together at the end.

That's not formula. Those are genre conventions.

NOBODY WANTS TO READ YOUR SH*T, P. 63

Remember at the start of this year when we were talking about the Foolscap Method—the writer's trick of outlining her story on a single sheet of paper?

The first item we cited was GENRE.

What *kind of story* are we telling?

We did this because we understood that once we knew what genre we were working in, we had a template of conventions and obligatory scenes that would guide us through every phase of the writing.

STANLEY AND ME AT THE CINEPLEX

My screenwriting partner and I always wanted to do a film noir. Both of us, for some demented reason, wanted to write a movie that featured night streets slick with rain, women who could plausibly be called "dames," and a climax where one of the lovers plugs the other with a .45 and a cynical quip.

How did Stanley and I prepare ourselves for this enterprise?

We went to the Aero (or the Laemmle or the Fine Arts or the Nuart on Pico) and bought tickets to *Elevator to the Gallows* and *Bob le Flambeur* and *Le Samouraï*. Not to mention *The Maltese Falcon, Out of the Past*, and *Farewell, My Lovely*.

We weren't just watching these films. We were studying them.

We studied them to learn the conventions of the film noir genre.

UNPUBLISHED BLACK IRISH JAB, "GO BACK TO GENRE"

I know, I know. This section of the book is about Act Two.

Bear with me.

Genre and genre conventions will be critical to the way we dig ourselves out of the Big Crash we have gotten ourselves into in our own second act.

Day 229
THE WRITER MUST KNOW
WHAT GENRE SHE IS WORKING IN

A story is experienced by the reader on the level of the soul. And the soul has a universal structure of narrative receptors.

Jung was right. There is a collective unconscious. Joseph Campbell was right. Myths and legends do constitute the fabric of the Self.

NOBODY WANTS TO READ YOUR SH*T, P. 63–64

If you and I are writing a love story, we would be crazy not to study *Pride and Prejudice* and *When Harry Met Sally* and *Annie Hall*. Why? So we can define for ourselves the iron-clad "must-haves" of a romance. Among others:

1. There must be a "meet cute."

2. The lovers must part in Act Two, seemingly forever, before they come together again at the story's climax.

3. There must a plausible rival for our principals' affections.

Don't believe me? Watch *Romeo and Juliet* or *Silver Linings Playbook* or *Shakespeare in Love*.

STEVEN PRESSFIELD

Day 230
GENRE AND MY BIG CRASH

Have you ever wondered what an editor does? (I mean beyond acquisition and branding and marketing.)

An editor *understands genre*.

Shawn's notes to me literally spelled out the conventions of the genre I was working in—the supernatural thriller, sub-genre Devil Story.

BLACK IRISH JAB #13, "STARTING OVER, PART TWO"

Yes, it's true. I have been working for over forty years as a writer. And indeed it's a fact that in this case:

1. I had no idea what genre I was working in.

2. I had only the vaguest—and woefully incomplete—knowledge of the conventions of that genre.

No wonder *36 Righteous Men* was sinking like a stone.

Day 231
GO BACK TO GENRE

What saved me was *going back to genre*.

Specifically:

One convention of a supernatural thriller/Devil story is that the Evil One must be conducted into the material world by a female.

This was nowhere in my original story. I had no scene like that, no sequence, not even a shred of a glimmer.

Yet that convention was present, big as life, in *The Exorcist*.

It could not have been more obvious in *Rosemary's Baby*.

Why hadn't I seen it? Why hadn't I implemented it?

BLACK IRISH JAB #13, "STARTING OVER, PART TWO,

There are rules, Shawn was (gently) telling me, that you, the writer, cannot break.

Learn those rules and adhere to them.

STEVEN PRESSFIELD

WEEK THIRTY-FOUR

THE ALL IS LOST MOMENT

Day 232
THE ALL IS LOST MOMENT

In the screenwriting trade, there's a story beat called the All Is Lost Moment. This is our protagonist's darkest hour, the moment when he or she is furthest from their goal.

The All Is Lost Moment comes at the end of Act Two, about three-quarters of the way through the movie.

Look for it. Minute 72 to minute 78. It'll be there.

NOBODY WANTS TO READ YOUR SH*T, P. 104

Sounds like some horrible Hollywood formula, doesn't it?

It's not.

It's a station stop on the hero's journey.

It's real life.

It's how our personal odysseys actually unfold, and if you don't believe me, sit for twenty minutes in the back at any AA meeting.

Day 233
GIVE YOUR HERO
A GREAT ALL IS LOST MOMENT

Why is the All Is Lost Moment so important?

Because the darker the hero or heroine's hour, the more powerful will be their ultimate triumph/salvation/resolution—and the more emotional will be the audience's identification and involvement with him or her.

In the All Is Lost Moment, the Gal knows for sure she'll never get the Guy. The Drunk is certain he cannot beat his dependence on alcohol. The Compassionate UN Dude knows he has no chance of holding back the Zombie Apocalypse.

Life is like that, isn't it?

That's why we in the audience can relate.

How many All Is Lost Moments have we ourselves had?

NOBODY WANTS TO READ YOUR SH*T, P.104

Your job as a writer is to give your hero the deepest, darkest, most hellacious All Is Lost Moment—and then find a way out for her.

It's the night before the Big Fight. Rocky's in bed with Adrian. He can't sleep.

He gets up and goes downtown, alone, to the arena where he will fight tomorrow for the heavyweight championship of the world.

Until that moment, Rocky had been so psyched up by the success of his training and the support of his fans that he really believed he had a shot at beating the champ. Now, surveying the arena, dwarfed by the scale of the scene and the magnitude of the event, reality hits him like a knockout punch.

Rocky trudges home and crawls back in bed beside Adrian.

> ROCKY
> I can't do it. I can't beat him. I been out
> walkin' around, thinkin'. Who am I kid-
> din'? I ain't even in this guy's league.

UNPUBLISHED BLACK IRISH JAB, "THE ALL IS LOST MOMENT"

This is my favorite moment in one of my favorite films. Why? Because it's so true.

IN THE ALL IS LOST MOMENT, THE HERO HITS THE WALL

In *Chinatown,* Jake Gittes' (Jack Nicholson) All Is Lost Moment comes when Evelyn Mulwray (Faye Dunaway) blurts out, as Jake slaps her across the face, "She's my sister! She's my daughter!"

At that moment, Jake realizes the scale of the evil he is up against and has been up against, without realizing it, throughout the story.

Like Rocky, Jake understands now that he is way out of his league.

UNPUBLISHED BLACK IRISH JAB, "THE ALL IS LOST MOMENT"

In both *Rocky* and *Chinatown,* the hero thought he understood his situation. He imagined he grasped the scale of the forces arrayed against him.

In the All Is Lost Moment, the hero realizes he has misapprehended everything. He is not the person he thought he was, and he is not up against the enemy he believed he was. Our hero realizes he is outmanned, outnumbered, outgunned.

In his mind he concludes he has no chance to prevail.

Day 236
IN THE ALL IS LOST MOMENT, THE EGO FAILS

Breaker Morant is a classic 1980 Australian film, directed by Bruce Beresford, about three Aussie officers in the Boer War accused of shooting prisoners. It's a courtroom drama based on actual events.

The All Is Lost Moment comes when the deputy to the officers' supreme commander, Lord Kitchener, testifies at their trial and perjures himself, dooming the three to almost certain execution.

Up to that point, the three officers, Lieutenants Harry Morant, Peter Handcock, and George Witton (Edward Woodward, Bryan Brown, and Lewis Fitz-Gerald) had placed their hopes in court-martial justice. Now they see that the fix is in. The politics of a possible peace conference supersede all judicial integrity. The Bigger Picture makes the sacrifice of these three men inevitable.

UNPUBLISHED BLACK IRISH JAB, "THE ALL IS LOST MOMENT"

In the All Is Lost Moment, our hero (or heroes) must reconceive everything—about himself, his predicament, about what possible action he can now take.

He must switch out of ego thinking and into something else.

THE ALL IS LOST MOMENT REDUCES THE HERO TO HIS CORE

In *Hidalgo*, Viggo Mortensen plays Frank Hopkins, the true historical long-distance horse racer. Hidalgo is Frank's unbeatable mustang pony. In the film, Hopkins and Hidalgo compete against the finest purebred Arabian horses in a three-thousand-mile race across Arabia, Iraq, and Syria in the last decade of the nineteenth century.

The All Is Lost Moment comes within sprinting distance of the finish when Hidalgo collapses from exhaustion, at the point of death. Hopkins literally has his .45 cocked, ready to put his beloved mount out of its misery. Hopkins himself is in a near-hallucinatory state from fatigue, heat, and dehydration.

In other words, our hero has been reduced to the naked core of his being.

UNPUBLISHED BLACK IRISH JAB, "THE ALL IS LOST MOMENT"

The purpose of the All Is Lost Moment is to break the hero down to his or her emotional, moral, and spiritual essence. This is where we and our readers find out what our protagonist is really made of.

Day 238
MULTIPLE ALL IS LOST MOMENTS

Sometimes the All Is Lost Moment comes in installments.

Our hero gets hit by one blow, then another, then another. Each moment is an elaboration on the earlier ones, and each takes him deeper into despair.

UNPUBLISHED BLACK IRISH JAB, "THE ALL IS LOST MOMENT"

The All Is Lost Moment is the moment when the ego realizes it cannot solve the problem by itself...the ego, meaning the protagonist's material-world, first-level self—the self that relies on reason, hard work, frontal assault, etc.

In other words, the self that is bounded within the "I" parameter.

The Epiphanal Moment, i.e., the solution to this dilemma, is the moment when the identity shifts from the ego to the Greater Self and evolves a response based on principles beyond those of the rational mind.

WEEK THIRTY-FIVE

THE ALL IS LOST MOMENT
IN OUR REAL LIVES

I've had many. Here's one from *The War of Art*:

I dragged out my ancient Smith-Corona, dreading the experience as pointless, fruitless, meaningless, not to say the most painful exercise I could think of. For two hours I made myself sit there, torturing out some trash that I chucked immediately into the shitcan. That was enough. I put the machine away. I went back to the kitchen. In the sink sat ten days of dishes. For some reason I had enough excess energy that I decided to wash them. The warm water felt good. A pile of clean plates began rising in the drying rack. To my amazement I realized I was whistling. It hit me that I had turned a corner.

Do you understand? I hadn't written anything good. It might be years before I would, if I ever did at all. That didn't matter. What counted was that I had, after years of running from it, actually sat down and done my work.

THE WAR OF ART, P. 49-50

I'm cheating citing this passage because it includes an Epiphanal Moment. (The All Is Lost Moment ends before the Smith-Corona comes out.) But more about this in a few more pages.

MY FRIEND LINDA'S
ALL IS LOST MOMENT

Linda is a successful lawyer in Los Angeles. Here's her Moment:

"I had finished a week of meetings in San Francisco and decided to drive back to LA, rather than fly. I rented a car and set out early in the morning, taking my time and enjoying the trip. Around Bakersfield I started getting tired. I decided to stop for the night.

"The next morning, I woke up in a Motel 6, in the same clothes I had been wearing the day before, with an empty quart of Jack Daniels on the floor beside me."

WRITING SEMINAR, NASHVILLE, 2019

Did Linda have a drinking problem? Up to that moment she would have emphatically answered no.

Day 241
DAVID BALDACCI'S
ALL IS LOST MOMENT

David Baldacci is the mega-bestselling author of *One Good Deed*, *A Minute to Midnight*, *The Last Mile*, and many more. The following moment is paraphrased from his own course on writing on www.masterclass.com.

Baldacci, like my friend Linda, was a successful lawyer. But his dream was to be a writer. He was in a movie deal that his heart was set on.

The deal fell through.

It was the fifth, or sixth, or tenth time this had happened to Mr. Baldacci. "My writing dream," he said to himself, "is never going to happen. I might as well face it. I'm never going to be able to leave the law and make a living as a writer."

In his heart, he gave up.

UNPUBLISHED BLACK IRISH JAB, "THE ALL IS LOST MOMENT"

In the world of fiction and movies, the All Is Lost Moment is followed by a breakthrough—a turnaround beat when despair becomes hope (or desperation that's the equivalent of hope) that propels the protagonist into action in Act Three.

We'll get to David Baldacci's epiphany in the section ahead titled The Epiphanal Moment.

ROSANNE CASH'S
ALL IS LOST MOMENT

The following excerpt comes, with permission from Ms. Cash, from her wonderful 2012 memoir, *Composed*.

"It was late in the making of [my album *King's Record Shop*] that I had a dream that changed my life.

"I was at a party, sitting on a sofa with Linda Ronstadt [who was a real-life hero of mine] and an elderly man who was between us. His name, I somehow knew, was Art. He and Linda were talking animatedly, deeply engrossed in their conversation. I tried to enter the discussion and made a comment to the old man. He turned his head slowly…and looked me up and down with obvious disdain and an undisguised lack of interest. 'We don't respect dilettantes,' he spat out, and turned back to Linda. I felt utterly humiliated and woke from this dream, shaken to the core."

TURNING PRO, P. 77–78

I love this story of Rosanne's because her mentor was inside her own heart. "Art" delivered the tough love. But "Art" was Rose herself, arising spontaneously from the core of her being.

Day 243
THE GODS AND
THE ALL IS LOST MOMENT

What does the Muse think when she looks down from Olympus and sees you and me experiencing an All Is Lost Moment?

She is delighted.

Not for herself. For us.

UNPUBLISHED BLACK IRISH JAB, "THE ALL IS LOST MOMENT"

When our pride is humbled, we are ready to listen. The wisdom we had rejected before, we are now ready to embrace.

Maybe we're not quite as talented as we thought we were. Maybe the competition is more formidable than we had imagined. Maybe the task before us is harder than we originally believed.

Maybe we'd better recommit ourselves and prepare to pay a higher price.

Day 244
MY SECOND ALL IS LOST MOMENT

I was living in New York, tending bar and driving a cab. (This is about six years after my first All Is Lost Moment...see Day 239 above.) I had just finished my third novel that I couldn't sell, couldn't even get my friends to read.

I was researching the best ways to hang myself. The only thing that held me back was I had nobody to look after my cat Mo.

UNPUBLISHED BLACK IRISH JAB, "THE ALL IS LOST MOMENT"

To repeat a thought offered earlier:

The reason we as writers give our heroes an All Is Lost Moment is because it's real life.

It's not formula.

It's a law of nature.

It's the reality of how our journeys play out.

Day 245
THE ALL IS LOST MOMENT IN NONFICTION

The War of Art is nonfiction self-help.

It has no obvious hero or villain. It possesses no characters that can be manipulated like those in fiction. It has no Act Two and no All Is Lost Moment.

Or does it?

NOBODY WANTS TO READ YOUR SH*T, P. 174

The hero of *The War of Art* is the reader.

The villain is Resistance.

The All Is Lost Moment happened in the reader's heart long before she picked up the book. It was the moment when she said to herself, "My dream is to be an artist, but I just don't have what it takes."

That nonfiction project you're working on? That memoir or biography or TED talk or Big Idea think-piece? Put it seriously under the microscope. You'll find a hero. You'll find an All Is Lost Moment. You'll find an Epiphanal Moment.

You'll find a way to structure it like a story and make it pop.

WEEK THIRTY-SIX

GIVING UP

"WRITING IS A BAD IDEA"

I got this note a few days ago from a writer named Kati Reijnonen. I didn't know Kati. I had never met her, had never had any contact with her.

Dear Pressfield and company,

I am a Finnish writer, just submitted my third manuscript to the publisher.

I have been reading Steve's blogs and also books. They are very encouraging and uplifting but I have to say I disagree with Steve.

I left everything to pursue my dreams [but] the situation is that at the age of sixty, I am broke. I have spent [everything I had.] It's all gone now. I have no idea what to do next ...

My Muse has left me. I feel sorry to have written this but what I have written is my truth.

"WRITING WEDNESDAYS," STEVENPRESSFIELD.COM, 2/12/20

I wrote back to Kati, asking her if she would let me print her letter for the following Writing Wednesday. I thought it might strike a nerve among the writers and artists who follow the blog.

It did.

Day 247
TOUGH LOVE

Martin responded to Kati's letter (see yesterday):

"Writing is never a mistake. Everyone can write and there is no reason not to. Most things we do for fun don't make an income. That doesn't mean we should not do them."

Tamlin: "When the crying on the floor is all done, stand up and get back to work."

Amy: "Amen."

Valorietta: "If you write for the sake of income, you shouldn't write at all."

"[Get] a job to pay the bills and support your writing. Every aspiring writer wants to write full-time, but [if] you choose to burn all bridges just to write, it's not only not smart. It's dangerous.

"If you want to write, you can write. You don't have to quit your job and put everything at stake to do it."

"WRITING WEDNESDAYS," STEVENPRESSFIELD.COM, 2/20/20

Wow. And that's just from the first seven of 147 Comments.

Day 248
WE FEEL YOUR PAIN

And yet many others wrote in empathy with Kati's distress. Here's Alex: "Lot of tough love in these comments, but 'get up and keep working' is a heartless response to such vulnerability…Gloss over Kati's experiences at your own peril. If you…want to dismiss it as self-pity…perhaps you lack the courage to be clear-eyed about the reality of the situation."

Here's ML: "One of my favorite authors, Ishmael Reed, says writing is fighting. I would add, it is fighting for your life. You have to somehow fight through depression and use it to get to the next level."

And Dorothy: "I'm seventy, I've got fourteen books under my belt, and I've never made a living from it. I see the stats from the self-pub hustlers and green envy can well up in me till I remind myself their game is not my game…if writing is part of who you are and you have something you want to say, I say go for it. Find a way. Don't give up…"

"WRITING WEDNESDAYS," STEVENPRESSFIELD.COM, 2/20/20

Normally a "Writing Wednesdays" post gets fifteen or twenty comments. This one got 147 and, as you can see, just about everybody could relate to Kati's pain.

Maybe there's a community out there after all.

STEVEN PRESSFIELD

Day 249
WE'RE ALL IN THE TRENCHES

Continuing the responses to Kati's "Writing Is a Bad Idea," here's Trevor. "Writing IS for everybody. Being a 'writer' is definitely NOT. You are a verb, not a noun. I wish you good luck."

From Gigi: "My heart aches for you. I too have felt the pain of what I thought was a failure. Please know this, failure is your path to greatness! Because you had the courage to follow your dreams, you have learned the cost. Writing another book is not a bad idea. It is a brilliant idea. You must press through this!"

And from George: "I thank you for writing what you did because while I am not in your exact circumstance, I too have failed and failed again while continuing to find a way to stake everything to bring my gift to the world. You may be broke and broken but you are not alone. Others out there are suffocating in the belly of the beast and may have been there for years. Your post gives me hope that I am not alone in scratching my way through the side of a whale."

"WRITING WEDNESDAYS," STEVENPRESSFIELD.COM, 2/20/20

I was really curious to see how Kati would respond to this outpouring. It must have felt to her like drowning in the surf and having a platoon of beachgoers drop everything and plunge into the waves to save her.

Day 250
KATI'S RESPONSE

This is Kati who wrote the letter:

Thank you so much for all your comments!

I sent that e-mail to Steve at 4 a.m., which of course was a bad idea.

But if there is someone out there, reading these words, feeling lonely and lost, I just want to say: you are not walking this journey of trials alone.

At 4 a.m., last week Wednesday, while staring at the bedroom ceiling, I decided to write a book about failing. Because failure always comes at the heels of success. It is an essential part of creative endeavors.

So please don't listen to me. Keep on writing, you guys—but not for success. Write to tell us your truth. Don't give up!

With love and blessings,

Kati

"WRITING WEDNESDAYS", STEVENPRESSFIELD.COM, 2/20/20

Sometimes people will write me long, heartfelt letters, pouring out their pain and self-doubt. When I write back, I often say something like this:

"Sit down and read the note you just sent to me as if someone else had written it to you."

What I hope will happen is that the writer will see both her own Resistance and the power and passion of her dream. I think that's what happened with Kati, when she read what people had written in, just for her.

THE WRITER'S HEART OF DARKNESS

Here's part of what I wrote to Kati:

Yours is every writer or artist's nightmare. It's in everybody's head all the time, whether they address it or try not to think about it.

My own answer is that of course the dream of making a living as a writer or an artist or entrepreneur is a tremendous long shot.

That said, the idea of following one's Muse is a lifelong enterprise, one that we are faithful to for its own sake and not for worldly rewards. That to me is not only an honorable and noble way to live but the ONLY way for many of us.

Are you familiar with Elizabeth Gilbert, the author of *Eat, Pray, Love* and other books? Ms. Gilbert says that at the start of her career she made a deal with her writing. She said, "I will never ask you to support me. I will always support you."

"WRITING WEDNESDAYS," STEVENPRESSFIELD.COM, 2/27/20

Kati did a great favor to all of us by letting out her *cri de coeur* and posting it in public. I thank her and every soul who responded.

The struggle is the same for all of us.

Day 252
THE FRUITS OF OUR LABOR

Krishna declared to Arjuna:

"You have a right to your labor, but not to the fruits of your labor."

It took me a long time to understand this truth...and even longer to accept it.

WRITING SEMINAR, NASHVILLE 2019

Can we work, you and I, for the work alone and not for whatever recognition or reward we hope to gain from it?

WEEK THIRTY-SEVEN

THE EPIPHANAL MOMENT

Day 253
THE MOMENT AFTER
THE ALL IS LOST MOMENT

What makes us change? I mean really change. In real life.

Almost always it's an intense shock, a blow so emotionally devastating that it wakes us up and makes us see, truly and for the first time, something about ourselves—something cataclysmically self-destructive or self-deluded, something we absolutely cannot live with—that we've never seen before.

In my case it was the realization that I had utterly failed at the one thing that was most important to me and that the fault was no one's but my own.

In Rosanne Cash's case it was the idea that despite all her commercial and artistic success, she was still in essence a dilettante in that sphere of her vocation—the writing and the creation—that she respected and valued most and to which she most passionately aspired.

UNPUBLISHED BLACK IRISH JAB, "THE ALL IS LOST MOMENT"

That moment of excruciating self-confrontation is the All Is Lost Moment.

But what happens *after* the All Is Lost moment? How does the hero "come back"? How exactly does she change?

THE NATURE OF EPIPHANIES

"I wriggle a seat in the sand [and] peer about the camp to the trucks and jeeps dispersed among the camel thorn…I am an ordinary Englishman, barely out of my university years. Yet here I sit, in the vastness of the [North] African night, surrounded by companions who could have stepped from Caesar's legions or Alexander's phalanx …

"At the same time, I realise I myself am not a warrior. Not like these fellows. I admire them. They are men of action, warriors and man-killers. I'm not.

"This apprehension is, paradoxically, the beginning of my true vocation as an officer."

LIEUTENANT LAWRENCE CHAPMAN IN *KILLING ROMMEL*, P. 174–175

"All genuine epiphanies," Chapman continues, "seem to follow this model: their defining quality is the relinquishment of delusion. The initial fear is that one has lost something. A cherished self-conception must be given up, and one feels diminished by it. This is mistaken, however. A person discovers that he has been made stronger by the jettisoning of this sham and disadvantageous baggage. In fact, he has become more 'himself,' by aligning his self-concept more closely with fact."

Remember Rocky's All Is Lost Moment from Day 234? When he realizes his dreams of beating the champ are self-delusion? Here's how he comes out of it.

> ROCKY
>
> ...it's true, Adrian. I was nobody. But that don't matter either, you know? 'Cause I was thinkin', it really don't matter if I lose this fight. It really don't matter if this guy opens my head either. 'Cause all I wanna do is go the distance. Nobody's ever gone the distance with Creed, and if I can go that distance, you see, and that bell rings and I'm still standin', I'm gonna know for the first time in my life, see, that I weren't just another bum from the neighborhood.

UNPUBLISHED BLACK IRISH JAB, "THE EPIPHANAL MOMENT"

See the shift in Rocky's self-conception and aspiration? The overthrow in his objective?

That's an epiphany.

That's a breakthrough.

That's the stuff of heroes.

Frank Hopkins' unbreakable mustang Hidalgo has collapsed from exhaustion and appears near death. Frank, in despair, cocks his revolver and prepares to put his beloved mount out of its misery.

Heat and fatigue have brought Frank as well to the end of himself. He's hallucinating. He hears a sound. Like drums. Like chanting.

Frank squints and sees, shimmering in the heat mirage, several figures of his Native American ancestors. By their postures, the spectral figures seem to say, "We are your spirit guardians. Take courage. You are not alone."

The images fade.

Hidalgo stirs.

Somehow the faithful pony rises. Frank mounts. The race resumes.

WRITING SEMINAR, NASHVILLE, 2019

The ego has failed, but the spirit has prevailed.

The spirit has prevailed, in fact, *because* the ego has failed.

IN THE EPIPHANAL MOMENT, THE HERO CHANGES

At the end of Act Two of *Breaker Morant,* the three Aussie officers are unjustly convicted by a court-martial. Morant and Handcock are sentenced to death by firing squad. They despise this verdict. Both are bitter and defiant. But that night, one of Morant's friends, Captain Taylor, visits Morant in his quarters of confinement.

> TAYLOR
>
> I can arrange a horse for you. Some of the guards are sympathetic. [Escape to] Portuguese territory. Get a ship from there. See the world.

> MORANT
>
> I've seen it.

UNPUBLISHED BLACK IRISH JAB, "THE EPIPHANAL MOMENT"

Throughout the court-martial, Morant had been battling desperately to escape conviction. Now in the Epiphanal Moment he accepts his fate.

His self-conception has changed. His aim has altered.

Morant's object is, now, to go to his Maker on his own terms, backing down from nothing and no one.

Day 258
"TRUST THE FORCE, LUKE"

Luke is piloting his X-Wing against the Death Star, trying to find the needle-in-a-haystack point of vulnerability in this evil machine. He's got his targeting computer up to his eye. But the tech isn't working! The moment is slipping away!

Suddenly Luke hears the voice of Obi-Wan Kenobi (who was killed earlier in the movie), coming from...where?

OBI-WAN KENOBI
Trust the Force, Luke. Trust the Force.

WRITING SEMINAR, NASHVILLE, 2019

See the shift in consciousness? See the altered intention?

In this moment Luke truly becomes a Jedi knight.

A key corollary truth: The climactic action still remains.

Luke still has to dodge the enemy defenders. He still has to fire his weapons. He still has to hit the target.

The Epiphanal Moment launches us into Act Three.

The All Is Lost Moment of *The French Connection* comes after Popeye Doyle (Gene Hackman) and his partner Cloudy (Roy Scheider) along with police mechanic Irv (Irving Abrahams) have torn the Bad Guy's Lincoln Continental apart and still haven't found the heroin they know is hidden somewhere in the vehicle.

Until Cloudy asks Irv what the car weighed when he logged it in. Irv gives a figure. Cloudy checks the vehicle's manual. He cites a figure three hundred pounds lighter.

> IRV
>
> I've checked everything except the rocker panels!
>
> POPEYE
>
> C'mon, Irv…what the hell's that?!

UNPUBLISHED BLACK IRISH JAB, "THE EPIPHANAL MOMENT"

Popeye and Irv break open the rocker panels. *Voila!* The white powder!

But the movie isn't over. All of Act Three remains. The trap. The chase. The shootout.

The Epiphanal Moment launches the story into Act Three.

WEEK THIRTY-EIGHT

THE EPIPHANAL MOMENT
IN OUR REAL LIVES

Day 260
DAVID BALDACCI'S
EPIPHANAL MOMENT

The lawyer/aspiring novelist had given up on his dream of making it as a writer.

Where did David Baldacci go from there? (I'm paraphrasing from his masterclass.)

"I thought, 'I can't give up writing. It's too much a part of me. If I stop, I'll die.'

"So I'll keep going.

"I don't care if no one ever publishes my stuff. I don't care if I write for the rest of my life and my work never appears between the covers of a book. I'm not stopping.

"I'm a writer. I'm going to keep on writing."

WRITING SEMINAR, NASHVILLE, 2019

Again: the breakthrough consists of an acceptance of a new reality (even though that "reality"—that Mr. Baldacci did not have what it takes to succeed as a writer—ultimately proved false), succeeded by a revised resolution ("I'm a writer. I'm going to keep on writing") based not on others' expectations or opinions but entirely upon his own.

Day 261
MY FRIEND LINDA'S
EPIPHANAL MOMENT

Remember Linda from Day 240 who woke up in a Bakersfield motel with an empty quart of Jack Daniels on the floor beside her?

She drove back to LA and went to her first AA meeting.

UNPUBLISHED BLACK IRISH JAB, "THE EPIPHANAL MOMENT"

1. Acceptance of a long-denied reality. ("I have a problem with alcohol.")

2. Adoption of a new course of action (and self-conception) in the face of that new reality.

Day 262
ROSANNE CASH'S
EPIPHANAL MOMENT

Recall Rosanne's dream, in which "Art" turned to her with disdain and said, "We don't respect dilettantes."

That was Rosanne's All is Lost Moment.

Here's her Epiphanal Moment (from her memoir, *Composed*).

"From that moment I changed the way I approached songwriting, I changed how I sang, I changed my work ethic, and I changed my life. I went deeper into every process involved with writing and musicianship.

"I remained completely humbled by the dream, and it stayed with me through every waking hour of completing *King's Record Shop* ... I vowed the next record would reflect my new commitment. I had come to feel curiously like a neophyte in the studio after the dream. Everything seemed new, frightening, and tremendously exciting. I had awakened from the morphine sleep of success into the life of an artist."

WRITING SEMINAR, NASHVILLE, 2019

That's will. That's the product of the Epiphanal Moment. That's an artist taking charge of her destiny and her life.

STEVEN PRESSFIELD

MY OWN (SECOND) EPIPHANAL MOMENT

I was sitting in my apartment on 15th Street between Seventh and Eighth and I thought, "Instead of hanging myself, why don't I move to Hollywood?"

Until that moment my writer's dreams had all been about becoming a novelist. No other aim existed for me. It was Hemingway/Kerouac/Henry Miller or nothing.

Suddenly I thought, *What's wrong with movies? I love movies. I've worked in advertising writing commercials. I know what a camera is. I know what a storyboard is. I know what a script is.*

I've failed as a novelist. Why not head west and fail as a screenwriter?

WRITING SEMINAR, NASHVILLE, 2019

At once a tremendous weight fell from my shoulders. I looked over at my cat, Mo. He was ready to leave New York too.

Within six weeks we had packed and hit the road.

THE EPIPHANAL MOMENT
PRODUCES SHAME

Rosanne Cash writes: "I felt utterly humiliated and woke from the dream, shaken to the core."

This is not necessarily bad. In fact, I'd make the case that this kind of shame is good.

Shame wakes us up. Shame motivates us. Shame reconnects us to our flickering, nearly extinguished self-respect.

TURNING PRO, P. 86

In the post-epiphanal moment, we have two things going for us that we didn't have ninety seconds earlier. We have reality and we have humility.

And we have a third force working in our favor—shame. Why is shame good? Because shame can produce the final element we need to change our lives—will.

Epiphanies hurt. There's no glory to them. They only make good stories at AA meetings or late at night among other soldiers in the trenches. These soldiers know. Each has his own story, of that hideous, excruciating moment when it all turned around for him.

Day 265
EPIPHANAL MOMENT = TURNING PRO

There is great power in this [epiphanal] moment, for our characters and for ourselves in real life.

We've lost something, yes. A cherished self-delusion must be abandoned, and this hurts. But we have gained the truth. Our bullshit falls away. The scales drop from our eyes. In that moment we have two options:

We can reconstitute our bullshit.

Or we can turn pro.

TURNING PRO, P. 85

An epiphanal moment is a grounding experience. Our feet touch the earth. We feel solid ground beneath us.

The self-we-had-been seems like a different person. She is who we were. She is not who we are now.

In an epiphanal moment, we are reborn.

We were amateurs before.

Now we have the choice to become pros.

Day 266
EPIPHANAL MOMENT =
START OF ARTIST'S JOURNEY

In this moment, the hero experiences a breakthrough.

This breakthrough is almost always internal. The hero changes her attitude. She regroups. She sees her dilemma from a new perspective, one she had never considered before (or, if she had considered it, had rejected it), a point of view that offers either hope or desperation amounting to hope.

The movie now enters Act Three. The hero, fortified by this fresh hope (or desperation), charges full-tilt into the climax.

THE ARTIST'S JOURNEY, P. XIV

Our real-life Act Two ends with our acknowledgment of our true calling.

What will be the content of our Act Three?

If you're an artist, I can tell you right now.

Act Three will be you producing the works you were put on this Earth to bring forth.

STEVEN PRESSFIELD

WEEK THIRTY-NINE

A ROAD MAP OF ACT TWO, PART THREE

Day 267
ACT TWO STARTS WITH A "CROSSING OF THE THRESHOLD"

In Act Two, the hero leaves the Ordinary World and enters the Extraordinary World.

Huck bolts from Miz Watson's and sets out with Jim on a raft on the Mississippi.

Clarice Starling (Jodie Foster) takes temporary leave of the FBI Academy and accepts a special assignment from her boss Jack Crawford (Scott Glenn), helping to track down the serial killer known as Buffalo Bill.

Henry Miller leaves Brooklyn for Paris.

UNPUBLISHED BLACK IRISH JAB, "ACT TWO HORRORS"

Review time:

Is our Act Two still torturing us?

Are we lost?

Are we panicking?

Let's slow down for this coming week and recap what we've learned about the overall shape and structure of those scary pages that come between the Act One Curtain and the leap into Act Three.

Day 268
THE HERO ACTS ON AN INTENTION

Our hero acquires her intention in the Inciting Incident of Act One. In Act Two she pursues that intention.

Dorothy seeks the Wizard of Oz.

Esty Shapiro (Shira Haas) in *Unorthodox* flees her Chasidic community (and her husband) in Brooklyn and flies to Berlin, Germany. Her intention is to live as a free woman.

Mark Watney (Matt Damon), left behind on Mars, intends to survive until he can be rescued.

UNPUBLISHED BLACK IRISH JAB, "ACT TWO HORRORS"

The hero's intention is the reason he or she "crossed the threshold." To solve the crime, to find love, to expunge or expiate some act of wrongdoing.

But in Act Two, the hero comes face to face with a force he or she had only begun to deal with in Act One...the Villain.

Day 269
THE VILLAIN
OBSTRUCTS THE HERO'S INTENTION

Once the Alien is aboard the *Nostromo*, once the Great White Shark has appeared in the waters off Amity, once the *War of the Worlds* Tripods have burst from the earth in New Jersey, keep them front and center. The scarier the monster, the deeper the jeopardy, and the deeper the jeopardy, the more emotion will be produced in the hearts of the audience.

This works for abstract villains too, like the looming market crash in *Margin Call*. Once this monster has been introduced, the filmmakers go back to it again and again and every time the story gets tauter and the audience gets sucked in deeper.

NOBODY WANTS TO READ YOUR SH*T, P. 76

It may be an external villain like Doc Ock or Darth Vader. It may be a societal villain like racism in *Precious* or homophobia in *Dallas Buyers Club*. Or it may be an internal villain that exists entirely within the hero's head, as in *Silver Linings Playbook*.

But whichever form the villain takes, he impedes and frustrates at every turn the hero's efforts to achieve his or her intention.

STEVEN PRESSFIELD

EVIL DEEPENS WITH EACH CLASH
BETWEEN HERO AND VILLAIN

First it's the Alien alone, transforming itself and devouring members of the *Nostromo's* crew. Then it's Ash (Ian Holm), the science officer, who is revealed to be a robot aiding the Alien. Then it's the ship's computer, "Mother," and "the Company" itself, willing to sacrifice the lives of the crew to acquire the Alien for its Weapons Division.

The evil deepens with each successive clash between hero and villain.

UNPUBLISHED BLACK IRISH JAB, "BAD GUYS, PART FIVE"

Noah Cross (John Huston) in *Chinatown*. The serial murderer (Kevin Spacey) in *Se7en*. As the onion gets peeled back by the hero acting on his or her intention, the depth and power of the villain (or the levels of villainy) is revealed to extend deeper and deeper.

THE HERO TAKES SIDES
AT THE ACT TWO MIDPOINT

When a typhoon strikes in Herman Wouk's *The Caine Mutiny*, the emotionally vulnerable skipper of the *USS Caine*, Captain Queeg, loses control of himself and puts the ship in imminent peril of foundering.

Queeg's executive officer, Lieutenant Steve Maryk makes a fatal decision before the *Caine* capsizes and goes under.

> LIEUTENANT MARYK
> I'm sorry, sir, but you're not issuing orders on
> this bridge anymore. I've relieved you. I take
> full responsibility.

> CAPTAIN QUEEG
> Mr. Maryk, you're under arrest! Left to 180!

Maryk orders the helmsman to come to (safe) course 000. The helmsman turns desperately to the Officer of the Deck, Ensign Keith. "What do I do?"

> ENSIGN KEITH
> Come north, Stilwell. Mr. Maryk has taken
> command.

THE WARRIOR ARCHETYPE VIDEO SERIES, 2020

The hero—in this case two heroes, Lieutenant Maryk and Ensign Keith—makes a decision from which he or she can never come back.

Day 272
THE HERO REACHES
AN ALL IS LOST MOMENT

Near the end of Act Two, the hero comes up against an obstacle (or the accumulation of obstacles) that blocks her completely. The Death Star's defenses cannot be penetrated; the lost love, Daisy, can't be re-captured; the Monsters of the Id are too powerful to be overcome.

WRITING SEMINAR, NASHVILLE, 2019,

The hero realizes that, as she is thinking now (and as she conceives of herself and her capabilities), she cannot win.

She is toast.

It's Game Over.

Day 273
THE HERO ACHIEVES AN EPIPHANY

The hero solves the unsolvable.

He changes.

Either his mindset is transformed such that his intention alters, as Rocky's new aim to "go the distance" against the champ. Or he accepts the unacceptable, as Breaker Morant does facing execution.

Or she rallies and calls upon heretofore unplumbed resources to confront head-on the Ultimate Obstacle that had obstructed her, as Rosanne Cash did in real life.

WRITING SEMINAR, NASHVILLE, 2019

Can you identify these beats (or something like them) in your Act Two?

It has helped me, more than once, just to have this checklist, this road map, as I struggle to make this damnable passage of pages work.

WEEK FORTY

"AM I AN ARTIST?"

Day 274
SELF-DOUBT IS GOOD

The counterfeit innovator is wildly self-confident. The real one is scared to death.

THE WAR OF ART, P. 39

Remember, when we hear the voice of self-doubt in our head, that voice is not us.

That voice is Resistance.

Its strength is equal and opposite to the power of our dream—of the work we wish to bring forth, the change we wish to effect in our lives.

The more Resistance we feel, the more powerful the dream inside us.

STEVEN PRESSFIELD

Day 275
BIG FEAR = BIG DREAM

Remember what we said about fear, love, and Resistance.

The more love you feel for your art/calling/enterprise, the more important its accomplishment is to the evolution of your soul, the more you will fear it and the more Resistance you will experience to facing it.

THE WAR OF ART, P. 71

Sometimes a young writer will ask, "I have so many ideas, I can't choose among them. What should I do?"

My answer: Pick the project that scares you the most.

Big Fear = Big Resistance = Big Dream.

CRASHES ARE GOOD

Crashes are hell, but in the end they're good for us.

A crash means we have failed. It does not mean we are dead.

A crash means we have to grow.

DO THE WORK, **P. 75 [HARDBACK]**

Crashes come when we're at the threshold of ascending to a higher level—of craft or of courage or of aspiration.

A crash is Resistance's way of terrorizing us, so we don't make the leap to that next level.

Sartre famously said, "Hell is other people."

In this case, hell is us.

Day 277
PANIC MEANS WE'RE GROWING

When we experience panic in the middle of a project, it means we're poised on the doorstep of a higher plane.

Have you ever watched a small child take a few bold steps away from its mother? The little boy or girl shows great courage...for a few moments. Then she realizes what she has done. She bolts back to Mommy.

That's you and me when we're growing.

Next time, the child won't run back to mama so fast. Next time she'll venture farther. Her panic was momentary, a natural part of the process of growth.

DO THE WORK, P. 76

I know it's tough to believe this when our breath is coming short and every nerve in our body is screaming, "Help!"

But remember the power of Resistance. It would not be hitting us this hard if it didn't sense that we were on the brink of something evolutionary.

The next step.

A higher level.

Keep breathing and hang in there.

Panic is good.

THE BIG FEAR AND THE LITTLE FEAR

When I began [writing *The War of Art*], Resistance almost beat me. Here is the form it took. It told me (the voice in my head) that I was a writer of fiction, not nonfiction, and that I shouldn't be exposing these concepts of Resistance literally and overtly. Rather, I should incorporate them metaphorically into a novel.

That's a pretty damn subtle and convincing argument.

The rationalization Resistance presented me with was that I should write, say, a story about war, in which the principles of Resistance were expressed as aspects of the fear a warrior feels.

Resistance also told me I shouldn't instruct or put myself forward as a purveyor of wisdom; that this was vain, egotistical, possibly even corrupt. That scared me. It made a lot of sense.

What finally convinced me to go forward was simply that I was so unhappy not going forward. As soon as I sat down and began, I was okay.

THE WAR OF ART, P. 30

In my twenties, I spent seven years succumbed to my own Resistance. That period scared the hell out of me. Going back to that place was the Big Fear for me.

Confronting Resistance was nothing compared to that.

Day 279
FEAR OF REJECTION

Fear of rejection isn't just psychological. It's in our cells. Evolution has programmed us to feel rejection in our guts. This is how the tribe enforced obedience, by wielding the threat of expulsion.

Resistance knows this and uses it against us. It uses fear of rejection to paralyze us and prevent us, if not from doing our work, then from exposing it to public evaluation. I had a dear friend who had labored for years on an excellent and deeply personal novel. It was done. He had it in its mailing box. But he couldn't make himself send it off. Fear of rejection unmanned him.

THE WAR OF ART, P. 87

There's a heartbreaking end to this story. My friend died. His novel was still in its shipping box, unsent.

Day 280
ACT/REFLECT

The writing/composing/idea generating process progresses in two stages: action and reflection.

Act, reflect. Act, reflect.

NEVER act and reflect at the same time.

DO THE WORK, P. 41

In writing, "action" means putting words on paper. "Reflection" means evaluating what we have put on paper.

We do the first with our right-brain, the second with our left.

The prime directive during the action phase is to turn off the reflecting capacity.

Write, don't think. Write, don't self-censor.

Get the words down first.

We'll have plenty of time to evaluate (and revise) later.

WEEK FORTY-ONE

PREDICTABLE RESISTANCE POINTS

Day 281
RESISTANCE STRIKES
BEFORE WE BEGIN

Many of us have spent years in this state. We've got a great idea. We know exactly how to execute it.

But we can't pull the trigger.

We can't sit down at the keyboard and start.

Resistance has beaten us at Square One.

We can't even get out of the starting gate.

UNPUBLISHED BLACK IRISH JAB, "PREDICTABLE RESISTANCE POINTS"

Resistance, we know, is overwhelming, relentless, unstoppable. But it has one weakness. It's predictable.

We know how it will hit us. We know what it will say. And we know when it will hit us.

Resistance's first shot is *before we begin.*

Resistance terrorizes us with the scale of the work that lies ahead, the difficulty, not to mention the (almost) certainty of failure and the calamity that such an outcome will visit upon us emotionally, psychologically, and financially.

No wonder we can't start.

Day 282
RESISTANCE STRIKES AGAIN
AT THE END OF ACT ONE

Somehow we do begin. We plunge in. We make a start.

To our amazement, we find a favoring wind. Momentum builds behind us. We're rolling.

Then one day (around the end of Act One) it hits us. OMG, what have we done? The enormity of the task before us strikes us again. Yeah, we've made a start. But can we keep it going?

UNPUBLISHED BLACK IRISH JAB, "PREDICTABLE RESISTANCE POINTS"

At this point, we are like the explorer who has just sailed out of sight of land. We peer to the fore: nothing but blue water. We squint aft: the same.

Set your clock by this moment. Resistance will hit us here every time.

Day 283
RESISTANCE HAMMERS US
IN THE MIDDLE

Act Two, we have said, is a killer. Herewith, a few words from one who knows:

"In the middle term [writes David Mamet in *Three Uses of the Knife*], the high-minded goal has devolved into what seems to be a quotidian, mechanical, and ordinary drudgery: now we are not trying to establish the Jewish Homeland but negotiating a contract with a stationer to supply the paper so that we may write fund-raising letters."

UNPUBLISHED BLACK IRISH JAB, "SECOND ACT HORRORS"

Moses led the children of Israel out of bondage in Egypt. But what happened when the multitude struck their own Act Two in the wilderness? They missed those three squares a day under Pharaoh. They wanted to turn around and go back to their chains.

Resistance hits hard in Act Two.

Day 284
RESISTANCE IS MOST POWERFUL
AT THE FINISH LINE

Odysseus almost got home years before his actual homecoming. Ithaca was in sight, close enough that the sailors could see the smoke of their families' fires on shore. Odysseus was so certain he was safe that he actually lay down for a snooze. It was then that his men, believing there was gold in an ox-hide sack among their commander's possessions, snatched this prize and cut it open. The bag contained the adverse Winds, which King Aeolus had bottled up for Odysseus when the wanderer had touched earlier at his blessed isle.

The winds burst forth in one mad blow, driving Odysseus' ships back across every league of ocean they had with such difficulty traversed, making him endure further trials and sufferings before, at last and alone, he reached home for good.

THE WAR OF ART, P. 18

The danger is greatest when the finish line is in sight. Be wary. Don't open that bag of wind.

RESISTANCE AT THE FINISH LINE, PART TWO

I read somewhere that Michael Crichton (*Jurassic Park, Westworld, The Andromeda Strain*), when he was coming to the end of writing a novel, began getting up earlier and earlier. He'd rise at six o'clock, then four, then two.

He was getting up so early he was driving his wife crazy.

Finally, he took a room in a hotel (the Kona Village on the Big Island of Hawaii, so don't feel too sorry for him) and did nothing but write till he had put his new book to bed.

"WRITING WEDNESDAYS," STEVENPRESSFIELD.COM, 8/19/10

There's a reason why Michael Crichton wrote bestseller after bestseller, and it wasn't just talent.

He understood when Resistance would strike.

He struck first.

Day 286
RESISTANCE STRIKES AGAIN
AT MARKETING TIME

Artists of all kinds are notorious for being unable to sell themselves and their work.

How many painters do we know who underprice their masterworks...or writers who refuse to go out on the hustings, to do podcasts and interviews, to reach out to reviewers and influencers.

I'm that way myself. After twenty-three books, it's still excruciating for me to put on my pitchman's hat and stand up for my material.

Why?

Resistance.

WRITING SEMINAR, NASHVILLE, 2019

Resistance doesn't slacken its assault even when we've beaten it in producing our work.

It knows it can still kill us if it can keep our stuff from getting seen.

Resistance saves its most furious attacks for the days and weeks after we've typed THE END.

Day 287
GLYCOGEN

Marathon runners know there's a phenomenon called "hitting the wall."

Somewhere between mile twenty-two and twenty-four, the body's store of muscle glycogen will run out. The runner's legs will turn to lead. The urge to give up will strike with overwhelming power.

What saves the runner is foreknowledge.

When she feels her knees turn to jelly at mile twenty-three, she doesn't panic. She tells herself, "Ah, this is the Wall. Relax. Keep running. In sixty to ninety seconds, the body's cells will shift their fuel source from now-depleted glycogen to fat. This horrible feeling will pass. I'll find my strength again."

UNPUBLISHED BLACK IRISH JAB, "PREDICTABLE RESISTANCE POINTS"

Before I plunge in on any project, I rehearse myself mentally for the Resistance points enumerated above.

Resistance is nothing if not predictable.

It hammers us at the same points every time.

WEEK FORTY-TWO

HEAVEN IS OUR ALLY

Day 288
"ETERNITY IS IN LOVE WITH THE CREATIONS OF TIME"

The visionary poet William Blake was, so I understand, one of those half-mad avatars who appear in flesh from time to time—savants capable of ascending for brief periods to loftier planes and returning to share the wonders they have seen.

Shall we attempt to decipher the meaning of the verse above?

What Blake means by "eternity," I think, is the sphere higher than this one, a plane of reality superior to the material dimension in which we dwell.

"Eternity is in love with the creations of time" means, to me, that in some way this higher sphere takes joy in what we time-bound beings bring forth into physical existence in our limited physical dimension.

THE WAR OF ART, P. 116

There is another dimension "above" ours.

I can't prove it. But I live by it every day.

This loftier dimension is involved and attached, in an explicit emotional and positive way, to what you and I do here on this humbler dimension.

STEVEN PRESSFIELD

Day 289
WAS THIS HOW BEETHOVEN WORKED?

By Blake's model, as I understand it, it's as though the Fifth Symphony existed already in that higher sphere, before Beethoven sat down and played dah-dah-dah-DUM. The catch was this: The work existed *only as potential*—without a body, so to speak.

Beethoven's Fifth needed someone. It needed an artist to bring it into being on this material plane. So the Muse whispered in Mister B's ear. Maybe she hummed a few bars into a million other ears. But no one else heard her. Only Beethoven got it.

The master brought it forth. He made the Fifth Symphony a "creation of time," which "eternity" could be "in love with."

THE WAR OF ART, P. 117

In other words, Blake agrees with the Greeks. The gods do exist. They do penetrate our earthly sphere. And their aim is to help us.

Or, more accurately, to use us as a medium to bring into material existence that which had existed only in the sphere of potentiality.

Heaven is our ally.

Day 290
A PRAYER TO THE MUSE

I started each morning over coffee with [my friend and mentor] Paul Rink. Paul was a writer. He turned me on to authors I had never heard of, lectured me on self-discipline, dedication, and the evils of the marketplace. But best of all, he shared with me his prayer, the Invocation of the Muse from Homer's *Odyssey,* the T.E. Lawrence translation. Paul typed it out for me on his even-more-ancient-than-mine manual Remington. I still have it. It's yellow and parched as dust; the merest puff would blow it to powder.

THE WAR OF ART, P. 111

I tend to think anthropomorphically. When I imagine something abstract or mystical, my mind translates it into something "human." I give it a face and a body.

The Muse to me is real.

I say my prayer to her every morning before I sit down to work. I say it out loud in dead earnest. I have been true to the goddess 24/7/365. And you know what?

She has always been true to me.

STEVEN PRESSFIELD

Day 291
GRAVITATIONAL FIELDS

A work in progress generates its own gravitational field. You, the artist or entrepreneur, are creating this by your will and intention, your love and passion. This gravitational field attracts like-spirited entities.

What entities?

Ideas.

You started with a few scraps of a song; now you've got half an opera. You began with the crazy notion to restore a neglected city park; now the lot has been cleared and you've got volunteers phoning at all hours.

Your will and vision initiated the process, but now the process has acquired a life and a momentum of its own.

DO THE WORK, P. 44–45

The un-indifferent universe has stepped in to counter Resistance. It has introduced a positive opposing force.

This force is the universal, immutable energy of creative manifestation, whose role since the Big Bang has been to translate potential into being, to convert dreams into reality.

Day 292
WORK = MAGIC

When we sit down day after day and keep grinding, something mysterious and magical starts to happen. A process is set into motion by which, inevitably and infallibly, heaven comes to our aid. Unseen forces enlist in our cause. Serendipity reinforces our purpose.

This is the other secret that real artists know and wannabe creators don't.

Just as Resistance has its seat in hell, so Creation has its home in heaven. And it's not just a witness, but an eager and active ally.

THE WAR OF ART, P. 108–109

The common conception is that an artist, particularly a writer, works alone.

Nothing could be less true.

You and I are agents of an energy and an intention that we cannot see or hear or touch but that is nonetheless present beside us at every breath. Its aims are more "ours" than our own, and it itself is more "us" than we are ourselves.

STEVEN PRESSFIELD

Day 293
"WHATEVER YOU CAN DO OR DREAM, BEGIN IT."

I have learned a deep respect for one of Goethe's couplets:
"Whatever you can do, or dream you can, begin it. Boldness has genius, magic, and power in it. Begin it now."

—W.H. Murray, *The Scottish Himalayan Expedition*

THE WAR OF ART, P. 122

When we conceive an enterprise and commit to it in the face of our fears, a crack appears in the membrane between Blake's dimension of "eternity" and our own.

Angel midwives congregate around us. They assist us, not just to bring forth the work or enterprise we hope to produce, but they aid us as well to give birth to ourselves, to that person we were born to be—the one whose destiny was encoded in our soul, our daimon, our genius.

Eternity, as Blake might have told us, has opened a portal into time. And we're it.

Day 294
THE HOUSE OF MY EVOLVING SELF

That house is my psyche. The new rooms are parts of me I have never, till I dreamt them, been aware of.

THE ARTIST'S JOURNEY, P. 113

I was asked recently, "If you were to give one piece of advice—and only one—to someone who was lost and struggling, what would it be?" My answer surprised even me.

I said, "Pay attention to your dreams."

When we say heaven is our ally, what we're talking about is that higher dimension that we access through intuition, through inspiration…and through dreams. Our dreams are messages in a bottle from a Self that knows us more intimately than we, on this material plane, ever can or will.

A dream changed Rosanne Cash's life—see Days 242 and 262— and it has many times changed mine.

WEEK FORTY-THREE

THE ARTIST'S JOURNEY

THE HERO'S JOURNEY
AND THE ARTIST'S JOURNEY

Our hero's journey, yours and mine in real life, is that passage of self-initiation that takes us, like Dorothy in *The Wizard of Oz*, away from our home, through trials and ordeals, and returns us, as changed beings, to our home again.

Like Odysseus we step ashore again at Ithaca.

Our hero's journey is over.

What now? What comes next?

What comes next is our Artist's Journey.

WRITING SEMINAR, NASHVILLE, 2019

In the hero's journey, we are lost.

In the artist's journey, we are found.

WHAT IS THE ARTIST'S JOURNEY?

The artist's journey, which follows the hero's journey chronologically, comprises the true work, the actual production, of the artist's life.

From that moment, the hero is no longer a free-range individual. As Rosanne Cash declared in her memoir, *Composed*:

> I had awakened from the morphine sleep of
> success into the life of an artist.

Everything in her life that is not-artist now falls away.
She is on a mission now.
Her life has acquired a purpose.

THE ARTIST'S JOURNEY, P. 28

On our artist's journey, we produce the works we were born to bring into being. We find our gift and we offer it. But something else happens along this path.

We find ourselves. We become who we always were, but had never been able to realize, had never found the power and the self-belief to bring forth.

What then are the characteristics of the Artist's Journey?

Day 297
THE ARTIST'S JOURNEY IS INTERNAL

I used to write at a desk that faced a wall. Friends would ask, "Why don't you turn the desk around so you have a view outside?"

I don't care about the view outside.

The book or movie I'm writing is playing *inside my head*.

Dalton Trumbo wrote in the bathtub. So did Winston Churchill. Marcel Proust never got out of bed.

Why should they?

Their journey was inside themselves.

THE ARTIST'S JOURNEY, P. 29

The odometer on my old Chevy van ticked over the six-digit mark so many times I can't remember them all. That was during my hero's journey.

Now on my Artist's Journey I barely drive to the grocery store.

THE ARTIST'S JOURNEY IS PERSONAL

The novels of Philip Roth are completely different from those of Joyce Carol Oates, as the works of both are different from those of Toni Morrison.

None of these authors, gifted as they may be, can produce the works that the others can. In fact, none of them can write anything except what his or her own gift authorizes, that which is unique to her or him alone.

THE ARTIST'S JOURNEY, P. 30

I can't write what you write, and you can't write what I write.

Each of us comes into this world with his or her own gift.

That's all we've got.

We can't change it. We can't trade it in. We can't copy another, no matter how hard we try.

Our job on the Artist's Journey is to find that gift that is unique to ourselves—and give it.

Day 299
THE ARTIST'S JOURNEY IS UNIVERSAL

And yet millions of people can read Philip Roth and Joyce Carol Oates and Toni Morrison and be touched and moved and illuminated by all of them.

What is unique to the artist is universal to the rest of us.

THE ARTIST'S JOURNEY, P. 31

Sometimes as artists we're advised to "do something universal." And there is definitely truth to that.

But when I'm reading your stuff, what I want is something that's unique to you and your gift alone. It doesn't have to be "personal" in the sense that's it's about your real life. But I want something personal in the sense that it's coming from your own love, your own passion, your own obsession.

And guess what? If you do that, it will be universal.

THE ARTIST'S JOURNEY IS SOLITARY

Yes, artists collaborate. And yeah, there is such a thing as "the writers' room."

But the work of the artist takes place not on the page or in conversation or debate, but inside her head.

You, the artist, are alone in that space.

There is no one in there but you.

THE ARTIST'S JOURNEY, P. 32

Let me rephrase that.

"There's no one *on the material plane* in there but you."

Your Muse is with you. She supports you, she sustains you, she inspires you. She will never leave you.

But you are the only one in that space who can strike a keyboard or execute a *plié* or edit a run of footage.

Day 301
THE ARTIST'S JOURNEY
LASTS THE REST OF YOUR LIFE

There is no other journey in this lifetime after the artist's journey (other than, perhaps, the transition to the next life).

Once you board this train, you're on it to the end of the line.

THE ARTIST'S JOURNEY, P. 48

The Artist's Journey is the hero's journey of the human race.

While we remain in a physical body, it is the Superbowl, the Tour de France, the only game in town.

WEEK FORTY-FOUR

THE ARTIST'S JOURNEY IS DANGEROUS

Day 302
THE ARTIST'S JOURNEY IS MENTAL

The sculptor may shape marble or manipulate bronze. The architect may work in steel and stone. But these materials are merely the physical embodiment of an image that the artist sees inside her mind.

The artist's medium is thought.

Her product is the fruit of the imagination.

THE ARTIST'S JOURNEY, P. 33

The Hermetic philosophers believed that the universe itself was mental.

You and I, the ancients averred, possess no material existence as flesh and blood. Rather we exist as thoughts in the mind of "the All," which was their term for God, for creation, for All That Is.

If the universe is mental, as the Hermetics believe, it can be altered by thought.

Alchemy.

Lead into gold.

All in the mind.

STEVEN PRESSFIELD

Day 303
THE ARTIST'S JOURNEY IS DANGEROUS

The artist, like the mystic and the renunciant, does her work within an altered sphere of consciousness.

Seeking herself, her voice, her source, she enters the dark forest. She is alone. No friend or lover knows where her path has taken her.

Rules are different within this wilderness. Hatters are mad and principles inverted.

The artist has entered this sphere of her own free will. She has deliberately unmoored herself from conventional consciousness. This is her calling. This is what she was born to do.

Will she come out safely?

THE ARTIST'S JOURNEY, P. 38

Hemingway, Elvis, Janis, Jimi, Michael, Prince. Was it booze or drugs that killed them? Was it fame? Was it excess?

Or is there something perilous in the nature of the artist's pursuit, all by itself?

WHAT IS THE ARTIST AFRAID OF?

The artist is afraid of the unknown.

She's afraid of letting go. Afraid of finding out what's "in there." Or "out there."

The artist is afraid of finding out who she is.

This fear, I suspect, is more about finding we are greater than we think than discovering that we're lesser.

What if, God help us, we actually have talent?

What if we truly do possess a gift?

What will we do then?

THE ARTIST'S JOURNEY, P. 95

Resistance takes on a new form when we pass from our hero's journey to our artist's journey.

Before, Resistance's main effort was to stop us from beginning our work, from finding our calling and launching ourselves in its pursuit.

Now, on our Artist's Journey, Resistance's aim is to stop us from fulfilling that calling, from becoming the artist we were born to become.

STEVEN PRESSFIELD

THE ARTIST GROUNDS HERSELF IN A DIFFERENT REALITY

On her Artist's Journey, the poet or dancer or filmmaker no longer centers her identity in her ego. She packs up and moves to a different quadrant of her psyche.

This new center is the unconscious, the Jungian Self, the Muse, the superconscious. Here's Henry Miller from *Tropic of Capricorn*:

"I didn't dare to think of anything then except the 'facts.' To get beneath the facts I would have had to be an artist, and one doesn't become an artist overnight. First you have to be crushed, to have your conflicting points of view annihilated. You have to be wiped out as a human being in order to be born again an individual. You have to be carbonized and mineralized in order to work upwards from the last common denominator of the self. You have to get beyond pity in order to feel from the very roots of your being."

THE ARTIST'S JOURNEY, P. 102

The moment Henry Miller is talking about is the finish of the hero's journey and the start of the artist's journey. It's the moment we hit bottom and turn the corner toward becoming our authentic self.

THE ARTIST AND HIS DAIMON

"[My daimon] is not me...but a creature to whom I am bound. It is as if this thing called Alexander has been twinned with me at birth, fully formed, and that I only now discover it, aspect by aspect, as I grow.

"This Alexander is greater than I. Crueler than I. He knows rages I cannot fathom and dreams beyond that which my own heart can compass. He is cold and canny, brilliant and ruthless and without fear.

"He is I, more than I myself, and I am indivisible from him. I fear I must become him or be consumed by him."

THE VIRTUES OF WAR, P. 67 [HARDBACK]

We play with fire when we launch ourselves upon the field of potentiality.

"Beyond this point," as the ancient maps declared when they reached the limits of the known, "there be dragons."

STEVEN PRESSFIELD

ON THE ARTIST'S JOURNEY, ALL ENEMIES ARE MENTAL

Fear of failure.

Fear of success.

Fear of the new, fear of pain, of loneliness, of exertion, of intensity.

Need for external (third-party) validation.

Self-doubt, arrogance, impatience, inability to defer gratification. Predisposition to distraction, shallowness of thought and purpose, conventionality, insularity, the need to cling to the known.

THE ARTIST'S JOURNEY, P. 39

None of these enemies is real in the sense that, say, a lion is real, or a man with a gun. All are products of the mind.

Day 308

ON THE ARTIST'S JOURNEY, ALL STRENGTHS ARE MENTAL

Courage.

Honesty, particularly with oneself.

Self-confidence, patience, humility, compassion for oneself and others. The ability to receive criticism objectively.

Curiosity.

Open-mindedness.

Receptivity to the new.

The ability to focus, the ability to defer gratification.

Will.

Mental toughness.

The capacity to endure adversity, injustice, indifference.

THE ARTIST'S JOURNEY, P. 41

None of the capacities listed above is necessarily innate, but all may be acquired by effort and force of will.

STEVEN PRESSFIELD

WEEK FORTY-FIVE

THE ARTIST'S JOURNEY
IS ABOUT SELF-DISCOVERY

Day 309
THE ARTIST'S JOURNEY
IS ABOUT SELF-DISCOVERY

I've read many times that art is self-expression. I don't believe it.
I don't believe the artist knows what he or she wishes to express.

The artist is being driven from a far deeper and more primal source than the conscious intellect. It is not an overstatement, in my view, to declare that the artist has no idea what he or she is doing.

The artist is not expressing himself. He is discovering himself.

THE ARTIST'S JOURNEY, P. 36

I wrote in *Do the Work* that one of my mantras was "Stay stupid."

I was warning against letting the rational mind second-guess (and thus self-censor) our loopy, mad, dumb-ass creative impulses.

The goddess knows what she's doing, even if we don't.

Day 310
WHICH SELF
IS THE ARTIST DISCOVERING?

Whom exactly is the artist discovering?

Is Dostoyevsky discovering Dostoyevsky?

Which Dostoyevsky?

Is Dostoyevsky discovering "Dostoyevsky"?

Or is "Dostoyevsky" discovering Dostoyevsky?

My answer is #4.

The artificial ego-entity that the world (and Dostoyevsky himself perhaps) believes to be Dostoevsky is discovering a deeper, wider, smarter, braver personage that has traveled across leagues and eons to reach this present moment and will continue its passage long after "Dostoyevsky" is gone.

The artist himself is disposable.

What endures is the Self he is seeking, which is not "himself" but himself.

THE ARTIST'S JOURNEY, P. 37

The "I" that writes our songs and books and movies is not the "I" that shops at Piggly Wiggly or takes a driving test down at the DMV. Its photo is not on our passport, nor is its signature on our checking account.

"Tell me who you are, Junah. Who, in your deepest parts, when all that is inauthentic has been stripped away. Are you your name, Rannulph Junah? Will that hit this shot for you? Are you your illustrious forebears? Will they hit it?

"Are you your roles, Junah? Scion, soldier, Southerner? Husband, father, lover? Slayer of the foe in battle, comforter of the friend at home? Are you your virtues, Junah, or your sins? Your deeds, your feats? Are you your dreams or your nightmares? Tell me, Junah. Can you hit the ball with any of these?"

THE LEGEND OF BAGGER VANCE, P. 113 [HARDBACK]

The process of self-discovery is one of subtraction, not addition. The artist strips away her "influences" and her exemplars, i.e., every concept of who-she-is that she has been employing all this time to avoid the terror of at last speaking in her own voice and being who she is.

When she has gotten herself down to nothing, she's got it.

THE ARTIST DISCOVERS HERSELF, WORK BY WORK

The artist discovers herself by the work she produces.
Who are you?
Dance and find out.
Sing and find out.
Write and find out.

THE ARTIST'S JOURNEY, P. 148

The mystery lies in this:
Where does the work come from?

Day 313
THE SURPRISE OF
FINDING OUR VOICE

Even if you haven't read any of [my] books, you can tell just from [scanning] the titles that they possess a unified voice and point of view.

Three critical points:

One, this voice materialized on its own. There was no plan on my part.

Two, the voice was an absolute surprise to me. It revealed itself book by book, year by year, obsession by obsession.

Three, I had no choice as an artist except to follow this theme and serve it, as it revealed itself and evolved over time.

THE ARTIST'S JOURNEY, P. 15–16

I wrote three unpublished novels and more than thirty screenplays before *The Legend of Bagger Vance* (and, right after that, *Gates of Fire*) seized me and compelled me to get them down on paper.

Different as these two are, I knew as soon as I started writing them that I was working from a source that I had never been able to reach before.

The "I" that I had thought I was, was not the "I" that I had now gained access to.

Day 314
THE SURPRISE OF
FINDING OUR SUBJECT

I wonder if Stephen King knew when he was a kid that horror, the supernatural, and speculative fiction would be his métier.

I can testify for myself that I had no clue whatsoever that I would be writing about the things I wound up writing about.

It's as though some Cosmic Assignment Desk, with access to our test scores and aptitude charts (that we ourselves have never seen) is suddenly calling us forward and with absolute authority handing us our orders packet.

The artist's journey is nothing if not full of surprises.

THE ARTIST'S JOURNEY, P. 107

I would go further. I would suggest that if our next acting part/dancer's role/start-up idea is not a complete surprise to us, maybe we should rethink taking it on.

Day 315
WHAT THESE SURPRISES MEAN

The artist on her journey opens the pipeline to the unconscious, the Muse, the superconscious. With this, every prior assumption flies out the window—who our parents told us we were, what our teachers imagined we'd become, even what we ourselves believe we are or will turn out to be.

The Muse tells us who we *really* are and what our subject *really* is.

***THE ARTIST'S JOURNEY*, P. 108**

In a way, it's a bit of a cruel joke that life plays upon us. It sets us down here on this planet as an already unique and fully formed individual, but it doesn't leave us a clue as to who that individual is.

That, we have to find out on our own.

WEEK FORTY-SIX

ENCOUNTER WITH
THE UNCONSCIOUS

Day 316
THE MISNOMER OF THE UNCONSCIOUS

The Unconscious (to use the term as Freud originally defined it) is unconscious *only to us.*

We are unconscious of its contents.

But the Unconscious mind is *not* unconscious to itself or of itself.

The Unconscious is wide awake.

It knows exactly what it's doing.

And it's pretty pissed off at being called "the Unconscious."

THE ARTIST'S JOURNEY, P. 92

I liken my own artistic trajectory (that is, the books and other writings I've produced over the years) to the track of a kite surfer. Have you seen this sport in action? It's like windsurfing except instead of a sail, the surfer is propelled by a kite (it looks like a parachute) that soars above him on the wind and pulls him across the water surface.

That kite is the Unconscious, the Muse, the Jungian Self.

I'm below, on the board, hanging on for dear life.

STEVEN PRESSFIELD

THE ARTIST'S JOURNEY
IS ABOUT ACCESSING THE UNCONSCIOUS

You can attend the Iowa Writers' Workshop, get a degree in Literature from Harvard, hang on your wall a framed MFA from the USC School of Cinematic Arts. You can serve in the Navy SEALs in Afghanistan, survive heroin addiction in East St. Louis. You can break your back at hard labor, break your heart in love, break your balls in the school of hard knocks.

None of it will do a damn bit of good if you can't sit down and open the pipeline to your Muse.

The artist's journey is about that.

Nothing else matters.

Nothing else counts.

THE ARTIST'S JOURNEY, P. 47

We study, we train, and we discipline ourselves. We apprentice ourselves to masters, and we immerse ourselves in learning our craft. All this is critical, indispensable.

But its ultimate product is the moment we forget it all and leap, arms wide, into the unknown.

Day 318
A CURRENCY OF THE HEART

I'm an American, and Americans have scant patience for anything that can't be reduced to a number (a sports score, say, or a sales figure). We Yanks feel comfortable in a world that can be cut and measured, boxed and shipped, extracted from the earth and hauled to market.

The artist's journey has nothing to do with that.

The artist on her journey will make everything up, including herself. Her creations will be fictional, apparitional, chimerical. And yet the artist is neither a fabulist nor a charlatan. She is not lying. She is not deceiving.

Rather she sees, with the vision of the imagination, what lies beneath the box scores and the market quotes.

She sees what is real and brings it forth so that others can see it.

THE ARTIST'S JOURNEY, P. 43

I don't mean to disparage numbers. The two highest arts, so I've heard, are mathematics and music.

A JOURNEY BETWEEN TWO WORLDS

The artist's journey is about linking the conscious mind to the unconscious. It's about learning to shuttle back and forth between the two.

THE ARTIST'S JOURNEY, **P. 94**

In the early days of the Rolling Stones, I've read, the boys would send Keith down to the basement with his guitar while they waited upstairs for him to return with a riff or a lick that they could build a song around.

I believe it.

The basement.

That's where you and I need to go.

THE ARTIST SHUTTLES
BACK AND FORTH BETWEEN REALITIES

Have you observed your mind as you write or paint or compose?
I've watched mine. Here's what I see:

I see my awareness (another phrase might be "platform of effort") shuttle back and forth, like the subway between Times Square and Grand Central Terminal, from my conscious mind to my unconscious, my superconscious.

In a four-hour working day, the writer shuttles between realities a thousand times, two thousand, ten thousand. So does the choreographer, the editor, the software writer.

This shuttling is her primary skill.

It's her bread and butter.

THE ARTIST'S JOURNEY, P. 111

There's an exercise in improv called "Open the Box." Imagine you're holding a white box in your hands. The box has a lid on it. The exercise is to take off the lid and discover (and report) what's inside the box.

Sometimes it's a diamond, sometimes a tarantula, sometimes a ham sandwich.

The thing is: there's always *something* in the box.

THE UNCONSCIOUS
AND THE DIVINE GROUND

In *The War of Art,* I related a story about a seminar I attended once, taught by Tom Laughlin ("Billy Jack"), who in his non-movie life was a well-known, if controversial, Jungian teacher and counselor. Tom Laughlin drew this schematic of the human psyche.

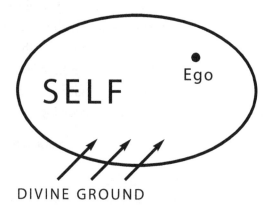

THE ARTIST'S JOURNEY, P. 125

If our intuition, our Higher Self, is wiser than we are (and I believe absolutely that it is), where does it get this wisdom?

THE CONSCIOUS MIND
AND THE DIVINE GROUND

1. This greater mind can be accessed by our lesser minds.

2. This greater mind *wants* to be accessed. It is actively reaching out to us, seeking our attention and participation.

"... the mystics, the gnostics, adherents of the grail and alchemists [writes John P. Dourley in *Jung and his Mystics*]...All these traditions share the sense that mind is natively imbued with the latent awareness of its universal connectedness. The development of this awareness intensifies the sense of the divine. This reconnection of the mind with its divine ground happens pre-eminently through the work of the dream and its symbols, expressing the energy of the divine."

THE ARTIST'S JOURNEY, P. 127

Is this line of thought getting too heavy?

Hey, this stuff is nothing but the same model of the psyche that every religion from animism to Zoroastrianism has been talking about for millennia.

STEVEN PRESSFIELD

WEEK FORTY-SEVEN

NOTHING NEW AFTER ACT TWO

Day 323
ALL CARDS ON THE TABLE

By the start of Act Three, all the game pieces should be on the board. Not just characters, but themes, ideas, emotions.

In *Casablanca* by the time the story highballs into Act Three, we've got Bogey, we've got Ingrid, we've got Paris. We've got the letters of transit, we've got Nazi Major Strasser, and we've got the plane to Lisbon.

The reader/audience should be asking, "How are all these pieces and motives going to come together?"

UNPUBLISHED BLACK IRISH JAB, "NOTHING NEW AFTER ACT TWO"

The axiom in movieland is "Nothing new after Act Two."

This principle applies to novels, dramas, and video games too. It applies to dance, to art installations; it even applies to restaurants. If our first courses have been guacamole with chips, carne asada with rice, beans, and tortillas, our Act Three better be flan or sopapillas or cheesecake chimichangas—and not Bananas Foster. (Though that does sound pretty good too.)

TWISTS COME IN ACT THREE

Going back to *Casablanca*, the action starts with us thinking Bogey is going to run away with Ingrid. But wait! Arriving at the airport, Bogey pulls a switcharoo. He tells Ingrid he's putting her on the plane to Lisbon with her husband while he stays behind to fight the Nazis.

But the twists aren't over. Suddenly SS Major Strasser comes forward and pulls a Luger. "No one's getting on that plane!" Wait! Bogey whips out his own pistol! He drills Major Strasser!

More twists. Captain Renault arrests Bogey! OMG, is all our hero's heroism for naught? But the suave Frenchman throws in another surprise.

> CAPTAIN RENAULT
> Someone has shot Major Strasser! Round up
> the usual suspects.

UNPUBLISHED BLACK IRISH JAB, "NOTHING NEW AFTER ACT TWO"

If you think these twists come thick and fast, watch the Derringer-in-the-Apple-Pie scene between Marlon Brando and Slim Pickens in *One-Eyed Jacks*.

Day 325
HIT THE ACCELERATOR

In my early days in Hollywood I worked sometimes with a producer I'll call Mark Gaskin. Mark had had two big hits, one in the action genre and another in the vein of "thinking man's thriller."

In our Third Acts I had a (bad) habit of trying to insert subplots.

"No, no, no!" Mark would literally rip the pages up and throw them away.

"This is Act Three. Floor it! Hit the accelerator!"

UNPUBLISHED BLACK IRISH JAB, "NOTHING NEW AFTER ACT TWO"

The rhythm of our story should change in Act Three. It should speed up.

Scenes should come quicker. Dialogue should be more clipped. Sentences on the page should literally be shorter.

BAM, BAM, BAM.

The reader wants to get to the climax.

Get him there.

Are you writing a Western? Make up your mind: The climax has to be a shootout.

Is your novel a psychological thriller? The clash at the finish must be between your hero and her own vertigo/claustrophobia/agoraphobia/arachnophobia/freak-out.

Is your story about zombies? Guess who has to appear, frothing at the mouth, in the climax?

UNPUBLISHED BLACK IRISH JAB, "NOTHING NEW AFTER ACT TWO"

I wrote a novel called *Killing Rommel*. It was about a British commando unit fighting against the German Afrika Korps in WWII. Will you believe me when I confess I was nine-tenths of the way through before it occurred to me, "Gee, maybe I should have a scene with Rommel in the climax?"

Don't be dumb like me.

If your story has the word "Terminator" in the title, the climax can be nothing but the hero versus this homicidal cyborg (unless we've got a Good Terminator, in which case it's him and the human hero versus the Bad Terminator).

Day 327
HERO AND VILLAIN
CLASH OVER ISSUE OF THEME

But hero and villain cannot clash in the climax over some random issue.

They must duel to the death (or at least metaphorical death) over the story's theme.

UNPUBLISHED BLACK IRISH JAB, "NOTHING NEW AFTER ACT TWO"

If it's *Apocalypse Now*, the clash must epitomize "the horror, the horror!"

If it's *The Godfather*, the climax must be about family.

If it's *La La Land*, the last look between Sebastian (Ryan Gosling) and Mia (Emma Stone) must be about the heartbreaking choices we make when caught between career and love.

Day 328
THE HERO DOESN'T ALWAYS WIN

Jake Gittes is devastated in the final scene of *Chinatown*.
Shane rides off with his dreams shattered in *Shane*.
Even Alvy Singer loses Annie Hall in the end.

WRITING SEMINAR, NASHVILLE, 2019

It never hurts the story to have the villain win. That decision simply empowers our story to make a different point.

How many times do heroes win in real life?

SOMETIMES THE HERO
ISN'T EVEN ON THE PAGE

From *Gate of Horn* by G.R. Levy:

"But Tragedy had learned from Epic that the mortal hero is often pitted against an invisible foe. In using heroic themes, Tragedy exhibits a duel no longer between equals but between man and a superior power. Therefore, defeat is essential, for the real hero is the unseen God, who forces the protagonist to conform to his own fate, his Idea, in order to fulfill his destiny."

UNPUBLISHED WORK SUCCEEDING THE ARTIST'S JOURNEY

Shane never had a chance of hanging up his guns when he entered the valley. Nor was it in the cards for Oedipus to live happily on the throne of Thebes. Or even for the Dude to get his carpet back.

The greatest stories have Unseen Forces as their heroes.

What makes them great (and tragic, in the truest sense) is that the human actor, in the end, comes to perceive these forces and offer up to them, at last, the respect and deference they deserve.

WEEK FORTY-EIGHT

THE MUSE

Day 330
WHO ARE THE MUSES?

In Greek mythology the Muses are nine sisters, daughters of Zeus and Mnemosyne (Memory).

Their names are Clio, Erato, Thalia, Terpsichore, Calliope, Polyhymnia, Euterpe, Melpomene, and Urania. Their job is to inspire artists. Each Muse is responsible for a different art.

There's a neighborhood in New Orleans where the streets are named after the Muses. I lived there once and had no idea; I thought they were just weird names.

THE WAR OF ART, P. 113

The classic image is of the composer at his piano (or the writer with her quill pen) while the Muse hovers at his or her shoulder, whispering inspiration.

Sounds quaint, doesn't it?

Trust me. It's 100% accurate.

STEVEN PRESSFIELD

WHERE DO IDEAS COME FROM?

The universe, the Greeks believed, was not indifferent. The gods take an active interest in human affairs and intercede for good or ill in our mortal designs.

The contemporary view is that all this is charming but preposterous.

Is it?

Then answer this:

Where did *Hamlet* come from?

Where did the Parthenon come from?

Where did *Nude Descending a Staircase* come from?

THE WAR OF ART, P. 115

Where is your next idea coming from?

Day 332
SOCRATES ON
POSSESSION BY THE MUSES

From Plato's *Phaedrus*, quoting Socrates:

"But if a man comes to the door of poetry untouched by the madness of the Muses, believing that technique alone will make him a good poet, he and his sane compositions never reach perfection, but are utterly eclipsed by the performances of the inspired madman."

THE WAR OF ART, P. 113

The ancients sensed powerful primordial forces in the world. To make these approachable, they gave them human faces. They called them Zeus, Apollo, Aphrodite.

Native Americans felt the same mystery but rendered it in animistic forms—Bear Teacher, Hawk Messenger, Coyote Trickster.

Our ancestors were keenly cognizant of forces and energies whose seat was not in this material sphere but in a loftier, more mysterious dimension.

STEVEN PRESSFIELD

Day 333
THE QUANTUM VERSION

Does it make you uncomfortable, my using words like "muses" or "angels"? You have my permission, then, to think of these forces in more scientific or academic terms.

Consider them as being impersonal as gravity or as "scientific" as the principles of quantum mechanics. Maybe they are.

THE WAR OF ART, P. 106

Maybe consciousness has no basis except in chemistry. Maybe time is an illusion. Maybe past, present, and future exist simultaneously in some million-dimension multiverse. I would not contest that.

Similarly, the call to growth can be conceptualized as personal (a daimon or genius, an angel or a muse) or as impersonal, like the tides or the transiting of Venus. Either way works, as long as we're comfortable with it. The point is that there are forces we can call our allies.

As Resistance works to keep us from becoming who we were born to be, equal and opposite powers are counterpoised against it, call them what you will.

The choreographer, for instance, may reach out to the neshama, asking, "What's my next dance? How do I solve this third movement?"

The painter calls upon the Muse in her own way, as do the filmmaker and the restaurateur and the software designer.

The office worker stuck in her cubicle may find herself turning inward for wisdom, asking, "Should I quit? Should I stay? What should I do?"

When we quiet ourselves and listen for that "still, small voice" inside us, what we're trying to reach is the neshama, the Muse. Our soul. Our Self.

THE ARTIST'S JOURNEY, P. 122

The soul, we feel certain, has the answers. It knows best.

Day 335
THE MUSE AND THE HERO'S JOURNEY

We've said that the artist's skill is to shuttle from the material sphere to the sphere of potentiality and back again.

Each one of those trips is a hero's journey.

Jay-Z in his studio may complete ten thousand hero's journeys a day. Ordinary world to Call to Crossing the Threshold to Extraordinary World and back again.

You do too. Watch yourself today as you bang out your five hundred words. You'll see the hero's journey over and over.

THE ARTIST'S JOURNEY, P. 66

When you and I were on our literal hero's journey, banging around the planet fleeing our own vocation and our calling, we might have thought we were wasting our time. We weren't.

Every ordeal of self-initiation we endured was to prepare us for the everyday miracle of opening ourselves to our Muse, of sitting down and doing our work.

Day 336
THE MYSTICAL AND THE MATTER OF FACT

The artist's journey is an alchemical admixture of the airy-fairy and the workshop-practical. On the one hand we're teaching ourselves to surrender to the moment, to inspiration, to intuition, to imagination. On the other, a huge part of our day is about discovering and mastering the nuts-and-bolts mechanics of how to reproduce in the real world the stuff we have encountered in the sphere of the imagination.

Monet spent years figuring out how to affix blobs of paint to canvas in such a manner as to produce the illusion of sunlight reflecting off the surface of water. Hemingway labored for years teaching himself to set simple word after simple word in such sequence as to reproduce for the reader the illusion of real events unfolding in real time before his eyes.

THE ARTIST'S JOURNEY, P. 69

Like an alchemist laboring to turn lead into gold, the artist operates simultaneously on the planes of the ethereal and the elemental.

STEVEN PRESSFIELD

WEEK FORTY-NINE

A MODEL OF THE UNIVERSE

Day 337
HOW THE WORLD WORKS

I'm going to attempt to sum up my conception of How the World Works, or at least how the artist's world works.

Can I back this up scientifically, empirically, intellectually?

Hell no.

Can I cite any studies, proofs, academic discourses?

Not even close.

Will you trust me anyway?

What follows, then, is my own personal, totally-unproveable, completely idiosyncratic Theory of Everything.

WRITING SEMINAR, NASHVILLE, 2019

What I base this theory on is nothing but my own experience over fifty years of facing the blank page and trying to figure out how to make that mysterious phenomenon called the magic of the printed word work.

STEVEN PRESSFIELD

Day 338
A LEVEL ABOVE THIS ONE

There is a dimension "above" the material.

This level is invisible, immaterial, incorporeal. On this level, time is not real. Space has no reality. Death exists only as an illusion.

We cannot touch this level or see it or measure it. We cannot visit it. We cannot command it or summon it.

But we can feel it. We can sense it. We "remember" it, though most of us cannot recall from where.

WRITING SEMINAR, NASHVILLE, 2019

The level above our material dimension is the level of potentiality.

It is that which is not yet, but which will (or may) be.

It is the future.

This level is the plane that you and I are seeking to access when we write, paint, dance, start a business, etc.

A COMPANION AT OUR SHOULDER

In the *Odyssey*, our shipwrecked hero struggles for ten years to return home after the Trojan War. What scholars sometimes overlook is that at his side for that entire ordeal stands the goddess Athena.

Jesus spoke to his Father all the time.

Martin Luther King spoke to Jesus all the time.

In the *Bhagavad Gita*, Arjuna speaks to Krishna.

In other words, in all these tales, a being on the lower level communicates regularly with, and receives divine counsel from, a being on the higher level.

That's the way the world works for all of us, and it's how it works for you and me as artists.

THE AUTHENTIC SWING, P. 70

For Junah, that intelligence is his caddie, Bagger Vance. But Bagger, as we know from the law of metaphor, *is* Junah.

When Junah stops struggling and becomes Junah, he finds his Authentic Swing and becomes his authentic self.

Day 340
THE NESHAMA

In Jewish mysticism, there's a name for this higher level. It's called the neshama.

The soul.

The soul may be "out there," above us or below us. Who knows? Or it may be "in here"—in the heart, the Jungian Self, the unconscious, the superconscious, the collective unconscious.

WRITING SEMINAR, NASHVILLE, 2019

It doesn't matter "where" the neshama is situated, if indeed it is "situated" at all.

All that matters is that it is.

It exists.

Day 341
THE NESHAMA REACHES DOWN ...

Kabbalists believe the neshama is constantly trying to communicate to us. The higher realm is reaching down, with positive intention, to the material plane.

Above every blade of grass, as we said in Day 39, is an angel crying, "Grow! Grow!"

WRITING SEMINAR, NASHVILLE, 2019

If you're an artist, the neshama is your Muse. It holds, like a shelf in a library, the works you will produce.

The neshama holds your body of work in potential.

Remember Blake's verse, "Eternity is in love with the creations of time?"

The neshama is eternity.

It holds your works.

It wants you to bring them forth.

And it wants to help you.

Day 342
... WHILE WE REACH UP

As the soul, the Self, the Muse, the unconscious/superconscious/ whatever is reaching down to us...we are reaching up to it.

In spiritual terms, that reaching up is called prayer.

In artistic terms, it's you and me *trying to get our next idea.*

WRITING SEMINAR, NASHVILLE, 2019

We said in earlier chapters that the artist's primary skill is the ability to shuttle between worlds, between dimensions of reality.

The writer, the painter, the composer opens herself to inspiration. Her skill—acquired, perhaps, through decades of effort—is to tune her receptors to the Cosmic Radio Station and listen to the music coming in *just for her.*

There's only one problem ...

Day 343
RESISTANCE

"There is a second self inside you—an inner, shadow Self. This self doesn't care about you. It doesn't love you. It has its own agenda, and it will kill you. It will kill you like cancer. It will kill you to achieve its agenda, which is to prevent you from actualizing your Self, from becoming who you really are. This shadow self is called, in the Kabbalistic lexicon, the yetzer hara. The yetzer hara, Steve, is what you would call Resistance."

RABBI MORDECAI FINLEY CITED IN *TURNING PRO*, P. 128

This is my model of the Universe, or, as I said, the universe *as experienced by the artist.*

Level One: the material world in which we dwell.

Level Two: the invisible dimension "above" us, from which arise all our ideas and insights, the books and movies we will write, the dances we will dance, the innovations we will bring forth.

In between: Resistance.

Our job: Get through our own Resistance to reach Level Two... and bring back as a gift to our brothers and sisters what we find there.

WEEK FIFTY

KEEP WORKING

Day 344
KEEP WORKING

Somebody asked me, "What's the best piece of advice anybody ever gave you?"

My first thought was whoever told me, "Nobody wants to read your sh*t."

Then I thought of when my friend Norm Stahl told me over lunch, "Steve, God made a single sheet of foolscap paper to be exactly the right length to hold the outline of an entire novel."

Both these gems have been priceless in my inner world.

But, when I thought about it, I realized that the best piece of advice anyone ever gave me came from my friend, the movie and TV director Ernie Pintoff.

"Keep working."

BLACK IRISH JAB #23, "KEEP WORKING"

Love fades. Fortune is fickle. Talent will only get us so far.
Keep working.

Day 345
KEEP WORKING, CONTINUED

"Keep working," Ernie said. "Don't turn anything down. Porn flicks, slasher movies, free stuff for friends. Don't get precious. You're young, you're learning. Keep working."

He cited three reasons:

"One, working means you're getting paid. Every buck means you're a working pro, you're toiling in your chosen field.

"Two, when you work, you learn. Everybody has something to teach you. A grip will show you something about lighting, an editor will drop some pearl about what to keep and what to cut. Even actors know something.

"Three, you're making friends. Some kid who's schlepping coffee today may be a producer tomorrow. An actress you do some free work for today may get you hired for a rewrite six months from now."

BLACK IRISH JAB #23, "KEEP WORKING"

I took a lot of jobs because of Ernie's advice, and I never regretted any of them.

Day 346
BETWEEN BOOKS

Writers sometimes ask me, "What should I do between books?" My answer:

There should never be a "between books."

Don't stop. Don't let go of momentum.

Myself, I want to be ninety pages into the next book before I finish the one I'm working on now. My aim is to move seamlessly from one to the other. If I knock off Book #13 on Tuesday, I'm deep into the trenches on #14 Wednesday.

Why?

Resistance.

Resistance loves it when we stop working.

BLACK IRISH JAB #23, "KEEP WORKING"

I have a friend at the gym who used to hang out with Jack LaLanne. He said Jack had a rule. "It's okay if you skip a day working out. But on that day, you're not allowed to eat."

Jack had another guideline: "Every day you skip takes six days to make up."

Stephen King writes three-sixty-five, including Christmas and his birthday.

Don't stop.

There should be no "between books."

Day 347
WORK IN REAL LIFE

I'm thinking of successful writers I know. Two were cops (both homicide detectives). A third was a lawyer. One female writer was a stand-up comic. Another left a corner office at a big New York ad agency.

Every reason Ernie Pintoff cited for laboring in the writing field applies to working in a real-world profession.

Be a cook.

Be a cowboy.

Work in a bookstore.

Work in a steel mill.

You learn.

You acquire experience.

You make money.

You make friends.

You're a professional.

I have a bunch of writer friends, female and male, who served in combat.

BLACK IRISH JAB #23, "KEEP WORKING"

How can you write about life if you haven't lived it?

Day 348
KEEP WRITING

The great thing about working as a writer (as opposed, say, to trying to work as an actor) is you only need a pencil and a piece of paper to do your thing.

Maybe you're not being paid, maybe nobody knows who you are, maybe no one will ever read, let alone publish or produce your book or movie.

But you can KEEP WORKING entirely on your own.

I have a closet in my office. In it are thirty-seven screenplays. Seven of them actually brought in money. That means thirty (six months of work apiece) were technically for naught.

But those scripts let me KEEP WORKING. With each one, I learned something. On some, I learned a lot.

If you have to take a gig driving for Uber or waiting tables at Hooters, it's okay.

Keep writing.

BLACK IRISH JAB #23, "KEEP WORKING"

Nobody can stop you from getting up at five in the morning and putting in three hours (or two, or one) pounding the keys.

When someone asks you what you do for a living, answer, "I'm a writer."

You are.

Day 349
WISDOM FROM THE OSCARS

When Steven Soderbergh gave his acceptance speech when he won Best Director for *Traffic*, he held up the Oscar and said, "This is for everybody who puts in one hour a day pursuing their art."

If you put in that one hour, if you KEEP WORKING, you are not a wannabe writer, or an aspiring writer.

You are a writer.

BLACK IRISH JAB #23, "KEEP WORKING"

My friend Mike McClellan is a partner in a big-time law firm. He has a wife and two daughters, not to mention a time-devouring second career in politics.

Nine years ago, he made the commitment to write five hundred words a day (starting at 5:05 every morning, before the family woke up).

Three years ago, his 733-page novel, *The Sand Sea*, was published.

1. It is terrific.

2. Mike is deep, deep into Book #2, with Book #3 of the trilogy taking shape right behind it.

One at a time, the hours add up.

Day 350
KEEP READING

Keep watching movies and TV. Keep studying stuff that works.
Study how Hemingway did it, or Tolstoy or Toni Morrison.

That's work.

That counts as work.

Books I love, I've read ten times. I've underlined them. I've scrawled notes in the margins. I've mangled their pages so badly I can barely close the covers.

Movies? I've seen *The Wild Bunch* and *Lawrence of Arabia* so many times I can quote them from FADE IN to END CREDITS. I've watched *Seven Samurai* in so many translations I can cite the differing subtitles and tell you which versions I like best.

That's not getting into the weeds. That's studying your craft.

BLACK IRISH JAB #23, "KEEP WORKING"

There's only one way to get good at anything.

Did I forget to say?

Keep working.

WEEK FIFTY-ONE

WHAT IF WE NEVER SUCCEED?

Day 351
WHAT IF WE NEVER SUCCEED?

I stumbled onto the website of a novelist I had never heard of. What I saw got me thinking.

The site was excellent. It displayed all fourteen of the writer's books. A couple had been published by HarperCollins, several others by Random House. The author was the real deal, with a body of work produced over decades.

I found myself thinking: What if this excellent writer had never been published? Would we still think of him as a success?

Suppose he had written all these same novels but had never been able to find a publisher. Suppose he self-published all fourteen. Suppose his books had never found a readership beyond several hundred or several thousand.

Would we say he had "failed"? Would we declare his writing life a waste?

"WRITING WEDNESDAYS," STEVENPRESSFIELD.COM, 9/21/16

It won't surprise you to hear that I would immediately answer no.

I would consider this hypothetical writer a success. I might even declare him a spectacular success. And yes, I would say the same if that writer were me.

STEVEN PRESSFIELD

Day 352
MY BRILLIANT CAREER

My own real-life career is not that different from the hypothetical writer we talked about yesterday. I wrote for seventeen years before I earned my first dollar (a check for $3,500 for an option on a screenplay that never came near getting made). I wrote for twenty-eight years before my first novel was published.

What, then, constitutes success for a writer? Is it money? Sales? Recognition? Is it "getting her ideas out there"?

Or is it something else?

"WRITING WEDNESDAYS," STEVENPRESSFIELD.COM, 9/21/16

A friend asked me the other day, "How did you keep going through all those years?"

I had two answers.

First, I wasn't failing every minute. I was either working on something that gave me hope, or I had found some sort of paying gig that at least kept me learning.

The second answer was the real one, though.

I had no choice.

There was no fallback position. No Plan B.

I had to keep trying.

Day 353
BEING IGNORED

If you're a working writer struggling to get published (or published again) or wrestling with the utility or non-utility of self-publishing, you may believe of me, "Oh, Pressfield's got it made; he's had real-world success; he's a brand."

Trust me, it ain't necessarily so.

I don't expect to be reviewed by *The New York Times*. Ever.

The last time was 1998 for *Gates of Fire*. *The War of Art* was never reviewed. My other ten novels never.

The Lion's Gate is a nonfiction account of the Israeli victory in the Arab-Israeli War of 1967. I couldn't even get a mention in the *Jewish Review of Books*.

I'm not complaining. And for sure I'm not an exception among writers or other artists.

"WRITING WEDNESDAYS," STEVENPRESSFIELD.COM, 10/31/18

Does it bother me? I'd be a liar if I said I didn't want to be recognized or at least have my existence and my work acknowledged. But as Garth on *Wayne's World* once declared of his own butt, "Accept it before it destroys you."

Day 354
MY YEARS IN THE WILDERNESS

In a way I was lucky that I experienced failure for so many years. Because there were no conventional rewards, I was forced to ask myself, "Why am I doing this? Am I crazy? What's wrong with me?"

In the end I answered the question by realizing I had no choice. I couldn't do anything else. When I tried, I got so depressed I couldn't stand it. So when I wrote yet another screenplay that I couldn't sell, I had no choice but to write another after that. The truth was I was enjoying myself. Maybe nobody else liked the stuff I was doing, but I did. I was learning. I was getting better.

The work became, in its own demented way, a practice. It sustained me, and it sustains me still.

TURNING PRO, P. 107

There's only one real answer to the questions above.
I write/paint/dance/act/compose because I have no choice.
As Linda Ronstadt has said, "I can't not do it."

"How bad do you want it?"

This is Resistance's first question to all of us. The scale below will help us answer. Mark the selection that corresponds to how you feel about your book/movie/ballet/new business/whatever.

Dabbling * Interested * Intrigued/Uncertain * Passionate * Totally Committed

If your answer is not the one on the far right, put this book down and throw it away.

DO THE WORK, P. 68 [HARDBACK]

I've said before that writing (or any pursuit in the arts) is not brain surgery.

It's not.

It's harder.

You have to want it more.

RESISTANCE'S TEST #2

"*Why* do you want it?"

1. For the babes (or the dudes)
2. The money
3. For fame
4. Because I deserve it
5. For power
6. To prove my old man (or ex-spouse, mother, teacher, coach) wrong.
7. To serve my vision of how life/mankind ought to be
8. For fun or beauty
9. Because I have no choice

If you checked 8 or 9, you get to stay on the island.

DO THE WORK, P. 68–69 [HARDBACK]

I can add nothing to this.

Day 357
"BACK OFF TO WHAT?"

One of my favorite dialogue exchanges in movies comes from *The Wild Bunch*, screenplay by Sam Peckinpah and Walon Green.

In this scene the gang's leader Pike (William Holden) has declared his acceptance of the fact that the days of robbing banks and trains are coming to an end. "We gotta think beyond our guns," he says. Then this, to his buddy Dutch (Ernest Borgnine):

> PIKE
>
> I'd like to make one last score and back off.

> DUTCH
>
> Back off to what?

UNPUBLISHED "WRITING WEDNESDAYS," STEVENPRESSFIELD.COM

"What" in Dutch's response is some imagined finish line or stage of success, beyond which the obligation to fulfill our calling recedes or even disappears.

The truth is there is no "what."

Your vocation and mine go on forever. We are in this for the long haul. We are in this for keeps.

WEEK FIFTY-TWO

WHAT IS OURS
AND WHAT IS NOT

Day 358
WHAT IS OURS AND WHAT IS NOT

"Never forget, Alexandros, that this flesh, this body, does not belong to us. Thank God it doesn't. If I thought this stuff was mine, I could not advance a pace into the face of the enemy. But it is not ours, my friend. It belongs to the gods and to our children, our fathers and mothers and those of Lakedaemon a hundred, a thousand years yet unborn. It belongs to the city which gives us all we have and demands no less in requital."

GATES OF FIRE, P. 35

The final beat of the hero's journey is a "gift for the people."

Odysseus returns from his wanderings, Dorothy comes home to Kansas, Bob Dylan steps off the bus in Greenwich Village.

Their gift arises from what they've seen, what they've learned, what they've suffered.

It doesn't belong to them. It belongs to you and me.

STEVEN PRESSFIELD

Day 359
A GIFT FOR THE PEOPLE

In the mythology of the hero's journey, the hero at the conclusion of her ordeal returns home safely from her wanderings. But she does not arrive empty-handed. She returns with an "elixir," a "gift for the people."

This gift is the product of the hero's solitary suffering. It may be wisdom or queenly command. It may come with fire or the sword, driving out evil forces that have infested the kingdom. Or it may come gently, as poetry or music that heals and restores harmony to the land.

You, the seeker, have at last returned home. You are an artist now, as you have always wished to be.

What gift do you bring for the people?

You will learn that, now, on your artist's journey.

THE ARTIST'S JOURNEY, P. 12

The point is that it *is* a gift.

Give it.

Day 360
THE WORKS YOU WILL PRODUCE

The hero returns safely at last to (_____), the place from which she/he started, by means of a (_____), bringing for the people the gift of (_____), hard-won from his/her experiences.

THE ARTIST'S JOURNEY, P. 9

If you're an artist, I can fill in the final blank for you right now. The gift you bring is the works you will produce.

STEVEN PRESSFIELD

Day 361
"FORGET KING, FORGET COUNTRY"

"Here is what you do, friends. Forget country. Forget king. Forget wife and children and freedom. Forget every concept, however noble, that you imagine you fight for here today. Act for this alone: for the man who stands at your shoulder. He is everything, and everything is contained within him. That is all I know. That is all I can tell you."

GATES OF FIRE, P. 355

We write for love. To give. To help, even if it's only to donate a laugh or a moment of hope or truth.

When you doubt yourself or your calling, remember that.

Do it for your brothers and sisters.

Day 362
ARE YOU A BORN WRITER?

Are you a born writer? Were you put on earth to be a painter, a scientist, an apostle of peace? In the end the question can only be answered by action.

Do it or don't do it.

It may help to think of it this way. If you were meant to cure cancer or write a symphony or crack cold fusion and you don't do it, you not only hurt yourself, even destroy yourself. You hurt your children. You hurt me. You hurt the planet.

You shame the angels who watch over you and you spite the Almighty, who created you and only you with your unique gifts, for the sole purpose of nudging the human race one millimeter farther along its path back to God.

Creative work is not a selfish act or a bid for attention on the part of the actor. It's a gift to the world and every being in it. Don't cheat us of your contribution. Give us what you've got.

THE WAR OF ART, P. 165

That's my story, and I'm sticking to it!

Day 363
A CAVALRYMAN AND HIS MOUNT

"A horse must be a bit mad to be a good cavalry mount, and its rider must be completely so."

THE VIRTUES OF WAR, P. 183

It's not like being an artist or an entrepreneur is a prudent career choice.

It's nuts.

I mean think about it.

I couldn't get my own mother to read my stuff, let alone pay for the privilege.

If you want a sensible career, be a brain surgeon. Be a power forward in the NBA.

Still you wanna be a rock 'n' roll star?

Then be like that horse.

Or better yet, like that cavalryman.

Day 364
PUT YOUR ASS
WHERE YOUR HEART WANTS TO BE

The great secret that every artist and mystic knows is that the Profound can be reached most efficiently by concentrating upon the Mundane.

Isn't that the principle behind yoga? We reach the spirit by manipulation of the flesh.

"Put your ass where your heart wants to be" means take the simplest physical step first.

Want to write? Sit down at the keyboard.

Wanna paint? Stand before an easel.

Wanna dance? Get your butt into the studio.

Want the goddess to show up for you? Show up for her.

"WRITING WEDNESDAYS," STEVENPRESSFIELD.COM, 4/17/13

This is the secret. There's nothing more to it.

BONUS WEEK FIFTY-THREE (NINE DAYS LONG)

HAVING A PRACTICE

There's a well-known Gunnery Sergeant who explains to his young Marines, when they complain about the meagerness of their pay, that they get two salaries:

A financial salary and a psychological salary.

You and I, as artists and entrepreneurs, receive two salaries as well.

The first might be called conventional rewards—money, applause, attention. That kind is fine, if you can get it. The problem is most of us can't. We bust our butts training and practicing and rehearsing and nobody notices, nobody even knows we exist. No wonder we sometimes feel like quitting.

Then there's the psychological reward.

TURNING PRO, P. 105

When we do the work for itself alone, we're like that Marine who sleeps in a foxhole in the freezing rain but who knows a secret that only he and his brothers and sisters share.

When we do the work for itself alone, our pursuit turns into something else, something loftier and nobler, which we may never have even thought about or aspired to at the beginning.

It turns into a practice.

Day 366
HAVING A PRACTICE

What is a practice anyway?

To "have a practice" in yoga, say, or tai chi or calligraphy, is to follow a rigorous, prescribed regimen with the intention of elevating the mind and the spirit to a higher plane.

A practice may be defined as the dedicated, daily exercise of commitment, will, and focused intention aimed on one level at the achievement of mastery in a field, but, on a loftier level, intended to produce a communion with a power greater than ourselves—call it what you like: God, mind, soul, Self, the Muse.

TURNING PRO, P. 108

Here's how Elizabeth Gilbert concluded her TED talk, *Your Elusive Creative Genius*:

"And what I have to keep telling myself when I get really psyched out about that is don't be afraid. Don't be daunted. Just do your job. Continue to show up for your piece of it, whatever that might be. If your job is to dance, do your dance. If the divine, cockeyed genius assigned to your case decides to let some sort of wonderment be glimpsed through your efforts, then 'Olé!' And if not, do your dance anyhow. And 'Olé!' to you, nonetheless…for having the sheer human love and stubbornness to keep showing up."

Day 367
A PRACTICE HAS A SPACE

A practice has a space, and that space is sacred.

When you and I enter that space, we leave behind all in ourselves that is common or ordinary or profane. At the threshold of the dojo, the student takes off her shoes. She bows to the teacher or to whatever tutelary spirit inhabits this space.

This space is soul-space. We show it respect.

TURNING PRO, P. 109

It's okay to laugh in this sacred space; it's fine to have fun. We want to play. That's what we're here for. But that laughter is real laughter. It's the laughter of children, or of the gods.

Day 368
A PRACTICE HAS A TIME

The monks in their saffron robes mount the steps to the zendo at the same hour each morning. When the abbot strikes the chime, the monks still their breathing and sit.

You and I may have to operate in a more chaotic universe. But the object remains the same: to approach the mystery via order.

When we convene day upon day in the same space at the same time, a powerful energy builds up around us. This is the energy of our intention, of our dedication, of our commitment.

The goddess sees this energy and she rewards it.

TURNING PRO, P. 110

My friend Jack Carr wrote his first bestselling thriller in Starbucks and Peet's and in alcoves at the public library. But he's the exception. What made it work for him was his intention was so strong, and his passion and his commitment, that he brought a permanent space with him like his own personal hot spot.

Day 369
A PRACTICE HAS AN INTENTION

When Stevie Wonder sits down in his studio at the piano, he's not there to mess around.

Stevie has come to work.

The 10,000 Hour Rule, made famous by Malcolm Gladwell in *Outliers*, postulates that the achievement of mastery in any field, be it brain surgery or throwing a split-finger fastball, requires approximately 10,000 hours of practice. But the key, according to Mr. Gladwell, is that that practice be *focused*.

It must possess intention.

Our intention as artists is to get better, to go deeper, to work closer and closer to the bone.

TURNING PRO, P. 111

My friend David Leddick was a ballet dancer at the Metropolitan Opera. He used to take classes from the celebrated teacher Margaret Craske, who had danced with Pavlova. Miss Craske's dictum was, "Leave your problems outside."

She meant, "Once you enter my class, I want you focused entirely on what we are seeking to achieve within these walls. Leave everything else outside."

Day 370
WE COME TO A PRACTICE AS WARRIORS

The sword master stepping onto the fighting floor knows he will be facing powerful opponents. Not the physical adversaries whom he will fight (though those indeed serve as stand-ins for the enemy).

The real enemy is inside himself.

The monk in meditation knows this. So does the yogi. So do the film editor and the video-game creator and the software writer.

TURNING PRO, P. 112

The sword master advancing into ritual combat has inwardly made peace with his own extinction. He is prepared to leave everything, including his life, there on the fighting floor.

Day 371
WE COME TO A PRACTICE IN HUMILITY

We may bring intention and intensity to our practice (in fact we must), but not ego. Dedication, even ferocity, yes. But never arrogance.

The space of the practice belongs to the goddess. We take our shoes off before we enter. We press our palms together and we bow.

TURNING PRO, P. 113

Even the peerless sword master, Miyamoto Musashi himself, entered the fighting square to learn as much as to teach.

Day 372
A PRACTICE EXISTS FOR ITS OWN SAKE

Yeah, we'd love to get rich and famous. And it's true, we must remain aware of the competition in the real world and strive to equal or surpass it.

But in the end, our practice exists for itself alone. The real rewards come from it and take shape within its walls.

WRITING SEMINAR, NASHVILLE, 2019

When we drive home with our Oscar or our Pulitzer, when the celebration ends and the last of our friends have departed, we will walk out alone to our studio, our office, our dojo. We'll stand at the threshold in silence and we'll feel the presence of our daimon, our neshama, our Self.

This is the place.

This is the worldly locus where the two spheres converge.

When our time in this dimension is over, we will ascend to heaven from here.

Day 373
A PRACTICE IS LIFELONG

The Spartan king Agesilaus was still fighting in armor when he was eighty-two. Picasso was painting past ninety and Henry Miller was chasing women at eighty-nine.

Once we turn pro, we're like sharks who have tasted blood or renunciants who have glimpsed the face of God. For us, there is no finish line. No bell says game over. Life *is* the pursuit. Life *is* the hunt. When our hearts burst...*then* we'll go out and no sooner.

TURNING PRO, P. 115

People sometimes eye me askance when I say I believe in previous (and subsequent) lives.

It only makes sense to me.

I won't finish my task in this lifetime. I have to go on.

STEVEN PRESSFIELD

SPECIAL THANKS

To Shawn Coyne, who backed this idea from the start, who said at once, "This book has to have illustrations, and they have to be by somebody really, really good," and who had the inspired notion to reach out to Victor Juhasz to deliver them.

To Vic himself, whose outstanding drawings make turning these pages fun...and made writing them a kick and a pleasure.

And to my better half, Diana Wilburn, who designed this book, interior and exterior, oversaw its production and marketing and distribution and who, per Aeschylus, "brought the fire that hath proved to mortals a means to mighty ends."

SARSAPARILLA MEDIA
(sass•per•illa)

My dad's favorite drink was sarsaparilla. He'd come home from work, look at my brother and me and say, "How about a glass of sass?" Naming this new company Sarsaparilla Media is a way of paying homage to my dad.